Kitchens

Your kitchen deserves the best in planning and design, for you spend some of the most important and rewarding hours of the week there. You can make it wonderfully personal, too — an eloquent expression of your taste and life style. Thanks to the wealth of options in appliances, in fixtures, in cabinets and in durable, decorative materials, you can create a workplace that is distinctly original in its detailing, yet fully as functional as the faceless, institutional-looking kitchens of old.

Customizing can be as simple as imposing a better order on the way you store pots, cutlery, condiments and staples to suit your kind of cooking. It can be as innovative as a bold treatment of wall, floor or ceiling surfaces that gives coherence to a once disjointed space. And it can be as practical as installing new lighting, additional cabinets, or perhaps a service island — any of which could improve your performance and pleasure in the kitchen. What is more, even ambitious tasks can often be handled by the amateur who has a well-appointed toolbox and a modicum of patience.

Success in projects large or small lies with knowing what style suits you and applying that knowledge to the space and budget you have. The photographic prologue on the next eight pages is a sampling of kitchens in which form and function have been memorably wedded. In the text and pictures that begin on page 14, you will learn how to analyze your own kitchen needs, then how to go about executing projects that will make your goals a reality.

Crisp, efficient and compact, the kitchen above has all the best qualities of a well-run ship's galley. Cooking staples and little-used equipment are stowed in sleek banks of cabinets, but implements and seasonings that are employed frequently are in easy reach. Pans, for example, are hung from a clear acrylic rod, which has been drilled at the ends, fitted with steel hardware and affixed to ceiling joists.

The rustic kitchen at left is part of a barn conversion, and appropriately features natural wood from its beamed ceiling to its planked floor. But there is surprise, too. Storage cabinets above the counter have doors that are inset with contemporary stained glass. Hung in front of conventional windows, the colored glass glows with sunshine by day, and with hidden interior lighting by night.

Professional equipment, generous storage space, expansive countertops — all these signal that a serious cook resides here. Daytime light comes from the sun flooding

through windows and skylights; at night, spotlights in the hood over the stove and fluorescents above it provide a mix of task lighting and area lighting.

The roomy apartment kitchen above is the remodeled sum of what was a small kitchen, a pantry and a maid's room. To keep the space cozy and to separate areas for particular tasks — cooking, mixing drinks, menu planning and more — the designer has kept visual breaks, using portions of the original walls to create peninsulas of cabinets and counters.

The country kitchen at left cedes the center of the room to a massive harvest table with a full view of the fireplace, where embers glow invitingly and foods are grilled. A rustic étagère — crowded with jars and bottles of homemade preserves, pastas, herb vinegars and other delectables — is both handy storage and a culinary still life.

In the galley kitchen above, the pale green of plastic-laminate counters is matched in painted backsplashes and ceiling to unify a small space. Brighter colors blossom in the chintz chair pads of the dining area *(foreground)*. At the back of the room a window garden, lush with begonias, provides a visual grace note. Dimmers on every light provide quick scene shifts from one area to another.

Generous swaths of color wrap this spacious kitchen. Gray floor tiles, bordered by smaller pink and charcoal tiles, set the color theme, which is repeated in the gray plastic laminate of cabinets, in the coppery pink of glossy ceiling paint, and in the genuine copper of pots and range hood. Notable, too, is the way the utility column at right is turned to advantage, becoming the massive center post in an island of cabinets and extra work space.

Other Publications:
THE ENCHANTED WORLD
THE KODAK LIBRARY OF CREATIVE PHOTOGRAPHY
GREAT MEALS IN MINUTES
THE CIVIL WAR
PLANET EARTH
COLLECTOR'S LIBRARY OF THE CIVIL WAR
LIBRARY OF HEALTH
CLASSICS OF THE OLD WEST
THE EPIC OF FLIGHT
THE GOOD COOK
THE SEAFARERS
WORLD WAR II
HOME REPAIR AND IMPROVEMENT
THE OLD WEST
LIFE LIBRARY OF PHOTOGRAPHY (revised)
LIFE SCIENCE LIBRARY (revised)

*For information on and a full
description of any of the Time-Life Books
series listed above, please write:*
Reader Information
Time-Life Books
541 North Fairbanks Court
Chicago, Illinois 60611

This volume is one of a series that features home decorating projects.

Kitchens

by the Editors of Time-Life Books

TIME-LIFE BOOKS □ ALEXANDRIA, VIRGINIA

YOUR HOME

THE CONSULTANTS

Emily Malino is an award-winning interior designer. She writes a nationally syndicated column, ''Design for People,'' and is the author of the book *Super Living Rooms*. She is a member of the Architectural League and of the American Society of Interior Designers.

Florence Perchuk designs residential and commercial kitchens and bathrooms. She frequently writes about kitchen design and interior remodeling. A lecturer and consultant, she is a member of the American Society of Interior Designers.

Frederick L. Wall, a furniture maker and sculptor, is an instructor in furniture design at the Corcoran School of Art in Washington, D.C. His work has been featured in many exhibits and publications.

Library of Congress Cataloguing in
Publication Data
Main entry under title:
Kitchens.
  (Your home)
  Includes index.
  1. Kitchens — Remodeling — Amateurs'
manuals. I. Time-Life Books.   II. Series: Your
home (Alexandria, Va.)
TH4816.K593 1985   643'.3   84-8480
ISBN 0-8094-5504-8
ISBN 0-8094-5505-6 (lib. bdg.)

CONTENTS

Prologue • 1

The basic business of kitchen planning • 14

The preparation center 15
The cooking center 16
The sink center 17
Triangles that save steps 18
Tactics for major remodeling 19

Dressing up old cabinets • 20

Paint: A freshening finish 22
Painting perfect stripes 24
Stain and varnish to enhance wood's grain 25
New hardware: A change of accents 26
Decorative molding for doors and drawers 28
Spice racks on a door 30
A spice rack in a drawer 32
Concealed lighting for counters 33
Wiring lights in tandem 35

Crafting racks and shelves • 36

Fasteners to fit the job 38
Buying lumber 41
A wall rack from wood strips 42
Shaping a brass hook 45
A made-to-measure shelf gallery 46
Adjustable shelves for a window garden 50
The grace of curves from plywood and dowels 54
An overhead pot rack 61

A guide to new cabinets • 64

Corner configurations 66
Plotting a perfect layout 67
Installing base units 70
Adjusting counter height 75
Putting up wall units 76
An island that rolls 78

New work surfaces • 82

A ceramic-tile countertop 84
A simple layout for a straight counter 86
Three techniques for cutting tile 88
Tiling an old backsplash 90
The art of painting tile 92
Plastic laminate: Handsome and durable 94
Using a router safely 99
Special treatment for damaged counters 101

Paint and wallpaper • 102

Applying new color with brush and roller 103
Hanging a vinyl-protected pattern 108
Covering a soffit 113

Resilient tiles for the floor • 114

A checkerboard to stretch a small space 115
Laying tiles on the square 120
Designing your own tile floor 121

A selection of essential hand tools • 122

Power tools for ease and precision • 123

Acknowledgments and picture credits 126
Index 127

The basic business of kitchen planning

Designing a kitchen is much like tailoring a wardrobe. A clothes designer probes every nuance of an individual's practical needs and personal style, and from a pattern book selects the appropriate elements. Then, by a judicious choice of measurements, colors and fabrics, the designer melds the parts together. The result is a custom-made wardrobe adaptable to any occasion.

This volume is essentially a pattern book for kitchens. From dozens of decorating projects, you can choose those that suit your own culinary needs and visual taste. Old cabinets, for example, can be renewed by a gleaming coat of alkyd paint, by durable polyurethane varnish to highlight wood's natural grain, or by new hardware and moldings. You can improve cabinet function with ingenious ready-made storage devices or with homemade racks and shelves, and add new cabinets if need be. Worn counters can be covered with ceramic tile or new plastic laminate, or replaced with such varied materials as maple butcher block or synthetic marble. And you can enliven the whole room with intriguing new coverings for floor and walls.

Contractors can be hired to do any of these jobs, of course, but then you sacrifice some control of the work's design and of its quality and cost. This book seeks to provide a more flexible alternative. You can adapt the projects in these pages as you please, selecting materials, proportions and colors that suit your particular kitchen. And you can achieve professional results by doing the work yourself: Each project is spelled out in step-by-step drawings, often accompanied by a materials list itemizing needed supplies; in most cases, a drawing illustrates in exploded view how the various parts fit together; and a color photograph always shows the finished job. Using these aids, you can transform your kitchen into an efficient workplace and imbue it with your own distinctive style.

The beautiful kitchens shown on pages 2-9 illustrate two basic problems that confront any kitchen planner. A successful kitchen is first and foremost a culinary workshop, a room designed to meet cooking needs. However, the kitchen also is the social hub of many households: The family gathers there for companionship and conversation, and guests gravitate there to nibble, drink and talk. Planning for the social role, like most decorating, depends largely on personal taste. But functional aspects of kitchen design are susceptible to scientific analysis.

The first step toward a more rational kitchen plan is careful scrutiny of the current situation. List the sizes and contents of drawers. Measure shelves, noting the space devoted to china, pots and pans, staples and so forth. For counters, note how much space is devoted to general preparation and how much is adjacent to the sink, refrigerator and stove. From such figures, you can identify design shortcomings and devise better space allocations.

As well as fixing the old kitchen's flaws, you can tailor new features to the working style and social uses of the kitchen. If several cooks often work together or if you favor multicourse meals, you can expand counter space by adding an island cabinet with a butcher-block top. If you like to eat in the kitchen, you can reserve space for a table or a breakfast bar. A telephone often deserves a separate shelf, to forestall food-spattered messages; an extensive cookbook collection needs its own shelving, perhaps in a glass-doored cabinet. The possibilities are endless.

Before sketching an overall design, divide the kitchen into components called work centers, each of which contains work and storage space for a particular activity. This scheme, a basis for detailed planning, necessarily is a bit arbitrary because a kitchen's centers are interlinked elements in a flexible, personal enterprise. The three centers diagramed below and on the following pages — a preparation center; a cooking center, including a cooktop and one or more ovens; and a sink center — are the minimum. In elaborate kitchens, serving and refrigerator centers often are separated from the basic three; cooks who specialize in canning or baking may want to create separate centers for these pursuits as well.

The design of each center need not adhere to standard dimensions, which exist only for the convenience of the home-building industry. You can adjust the heights of countertops and wall cabinets (pages 75-77), and new cabinets can be custom-built to your specifications.

Tailoring kitchen dimensions to your needs is a province

of ergonomics, the study of relationships between humans and machines. Using the principles illustrated here, you can design each center to suit your height, reach and habits. The benefits can be dramatic. An early ergonomic study of hand dishwashing revealed that work at a sink whose bottom is about 32 inches above the floor — the ideal level for a woman of average height — requires only 80 per cent of the energy expended at a sink 39 inches high and less than 70 per cent of that used at a sink 26 inches high. Automatic dishwashers have obviated the drudgery of hand washing, but the sink's level still concerns cooks as they rinse dishes, scour pots and polish copper.

The ergonomically determined dimensions in the drawings below and on pages 16-17 provide for average cooks, but like all generalizations they are fallible. Many kitchens are too small to permit scientifically ideal dimensions. Ergonomic perfection sometimes must yield to visual harmony, so that adjoining countertops and cabinets have a single consistent height. And if your stature differs markedly from the norm, you may want to make kitchen heights depart from the ergonomic average.

You might determine ideal heights directly, by measuring such distances as the comfortable reach to a high shelf and by simulating different countertop levels, using a board set on blocks. Or you can calculate the heights mathematically: Wearing normal shoes, stand straight with your upper arms vertical against your body. Lift one forearm and, when it is horizontal, have a helper measure from the bottom of your flexed elbow to the floor. Then, to calculate the height for countertops, sinks and the like,

The Preparation Center

Overhead view. To accommodate ingredients, mixing bowls and small appliances, a counter should be at least 36 inches wide; the preparation center may adjoin the refrigerator or the sink, each of which requires 18 inches of added counter space. A standard counter is 24 inches deep, but this dimension is not critical: An average cook uses only the front 16 inches of the counter, and even with a straight arm can reach only 20 inches without leaning. The floor at the preparation center should include a 36-inch work zone, which allows for an open drawer plus the cook's body depth, and a 12-inch traffic passage; a full 24-inch traffic walkway (*below*) requires 60 inches of floor space.

Side view. At the preparation center, three heights are critical. Ideally, the countertop should be at least 6 inches below the cook's elbow — 32 to 34 inches above the floor, on average, considerably less than the standard 36-inch counter height — for greater leverage when kneading, chopping and mixing foods by hand. However, this lower height is less important for cooks who rely on electric mixers and food processors. Wall cabinets are usually located 18 inches above base cabinets (15 inches at an absolute minimum), for full visibility of the counter. A wall cabinet's second shelf should be no more than 69 inches above the floor, so even a short cook can reach it.

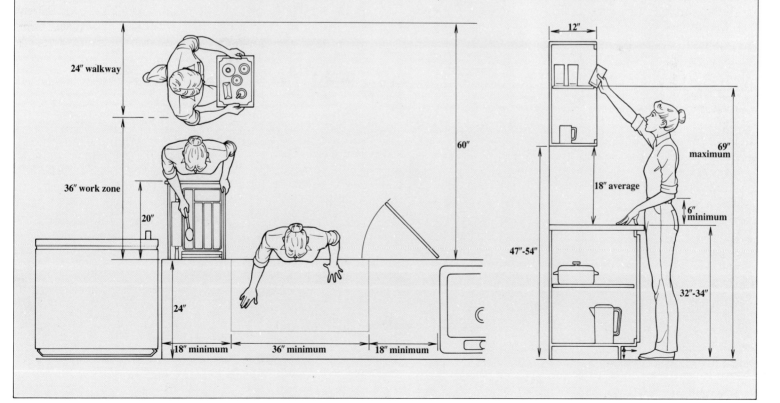

24″ walkway

36″ work zone

20″

24″

18″ minimum   36″ minimum   18″ minimum

60″

12″

69″ maximum

18″ average

6″ minimum

47″-54″

32″-34″

subtract from this measurement the allowance given in the captions for the side-view illustrations.

Once the overall dimensions of the various centers are decided, the last design step is ensuring sufficient storage space. Ideally, almost everything — small appliances, cookware, utensils and foodstuffs — should be located where it initially will be used. Often this system, called storage at the point of first use, can be adopted by rearranging the contents of old cabinets. Or you can add new racks, shelves and cabinets designed expressly for their contents. This first-use storage system involves some duplication of utensils, measuring cups and seasonings. But it is vastly more efficient than the traditional organization of storage by categories — pots and pans, staples and so

forth — irrespective of an item's intended use. In a study of the distance walked while making a simple meat loaf, the first-use system needed barely half the footsteps required by traditional storage.

The general principles of ergonomics and first-use storage govern planning for all kitchen centers, but each major center also has a few particular design guidelines:
● *The preparation center,* built around a large counter where uncooked food is sliced, chopped and mixed, should include storage for seasonings, baking ingredients, sauce ingredients and the like. Here also are stored the food processor, mixer, blender, mixing bowls, whisks, pastry tools, baking sheets, knives, cutting boards, roasting pans and casseroles. The refrigerator, with a cabinet

The Cooking Center

Overhead view. To provide ready parking for hot cookware, a cooktop (ordinarily 24 inches deep and 20 to 46 inches wide) should be flanked on one or both sides by at least 21 inches of counter covered with a heat-resistant material, such as ceramic tile. A separate wall oven or microwave (ordinarily 21 to 30 inches wide) requires its own 21-inch counter on one side. Since the combined depth of an open oven door and the cook's body consumes 40 inches, an oven or stove requires at least 48 inches of floor separation from the nearest obstruction.

Side view. The top of a stove ordinarily is about 36 inches above the floor, while separate cooktops that drop into counters can be set at whatever height is desired — a level of 34 inches eases stirring. Because a standard exhaust hood extends 17½ inches from the wall, the hood's bottom should be at least 24 inches above the burners, so that the cook can watch the contents of tall pots. On a wall oven, the open door's top should be about 4 inches below elbow height (36 inches above the floor, on average), a level that places the controls at eye level and allows the cook to lift heavy pans without strain.

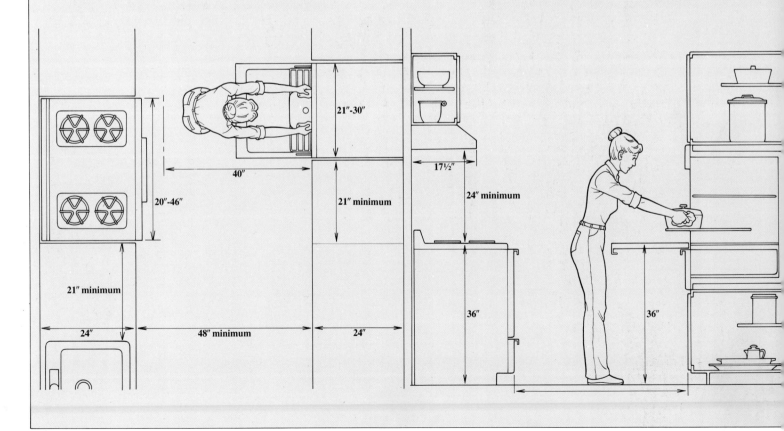

containing wrappings and freezer containers beside it, often is considered part of the preparation center.

● *The cooking center* can be built around a standard stove or a built-in cooktop and separate wall oven. The latter gives greater planning flexibility but takes more space. This center is the place to store ingredients that can go directly to the stove: Tea and coffee, pasta, rice, canned vegetables and such, along with their seasonings. It also contains pans that normally are not filled with water, such as frying pans and griddles; lids for stovetop cookware; and tools for stirring, mashing, measuring, turning, testing and carving cooked food. The cooking center usually is next to a serving counter, with tableware stored nearby.

● *The sink center* provides water for cooking, for washing food beforehand and for cleaning up afterward. Even with an automatic dishwasher, a double-bowl sink is useful because it allows both a 6-inch-deep bowl for everyday work and a 10-inch-deep bowl for washing large stockpots and roasting pans. Storage at the sink center contains foods that are combined with water before cooking, such as beans and canned soups; unrefrigerated foods that require washing or peeling; and cookware that is used with water, such as saucepans, colanders, strainers and the like.

Well-organized work centers deserve to be linked in a step-saving triangle such as one of those shown on the following pages. And once you have decided on an overall kitchen design, the techniques described on pages 64-69 will help you to draw it in scale, ready for execution.

The Sink Center

Overhead view. The critical sink dimension is its setback: the distance between the counter's front edge and the sink's front wall. This dimension should be as narrow as possible — surely less than 3 inches — to prevent shoulder fatigue. The sink needs a 36-inch-wide counter on one side to hold dirty dishes without stacking; the other side requires a 24-inch counter for a standard dishwasher or 18 inches for a rack of hand-washed dishes. The dishwasher's open door is the largest obstruction in the kitchen; allow at least 54 inches of floor separation from the nearest cabinet or wall, 70 inches if traffic must pass.

Side view. Although sinks usually are installed at the same 36-inch height as most countertops, ergonomic factors favor a rim roughly 2 inches below elbow height, about 38 inches from the floor, and a sink bowl 6 or 8 inches deep; a second, deeper bowl proves efficient for washing large cookware. The resulting 38-inch counter height is ideal for operations that do not require heavy labor, such as serving, straining foods, stacking dishes and the like. Wall cabinets should be positioned at least 22 inches above the rim of the sink.

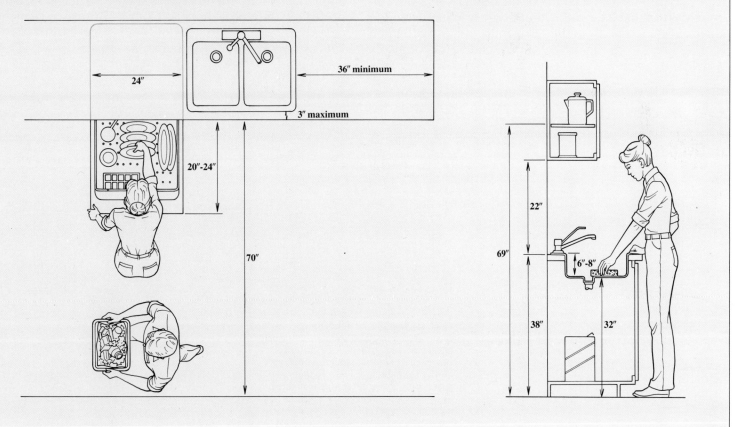

Triangles that save steps

Arranging a kitchen's work centers in a felicitous overall design is made easier today by decades of time-and-motion study of the work patterns necessary in cooking. Home-economics researchers have used the tools of industrial engineering — slow-motion films, stop watches, process charts and the like — to painstakingly analyze a cook's smallest motion. By recording each footstep on a floor plan of the kitchen, they have compiled flow diagrams for the preparation of everything from breakfast coffee to a four-course dinner.

The average cook, they found, spends more than one third of his or her time at the sink — filling pots with water, peeling vegetables, draining cooked food and rinsing dirty dishes — and another one quarter of the time at the stove; trips between these two account for most kitchen travel. The mixing center ranks third in time of use. Although work at the refrigerator occupies only one tenth of the cook's time, trips from the refrigerator to the sink and the stove are frequent. And the machinery of a modern *batterie de cuisine* — microwave ovens, food processors, blenders, toaster-ovens and the like — requires considerable counter space adjacent to each work area.

From these observations emerged the concept of a work triangle — with the sink, refrigerator and stove at the corners, and unobstructed paths along the sides. To balance the competing demands for long counters and for short trips between the three points of the triangle, its sides follow this formula: The sink should be 4 to 6 feet from the stove and 4 to 7 feet from the refrigerator; the stove should be 4 to 9 feet from the refrigerator. Ideally, the kitchen's

normal traffic path should route other traffic away from this triangle, to prevent collisions with the cook.

In a rectangular room, the work triangle generally dictates one of the three generic types of kitchen arrangements shown here — a galley kitchen, an L-shaped kitchen or a U-shaped kitchen — but each of these has innumerable variations. One of a triangle's sides may be a peninsula of cabinets, perhaps with a breakfast bar at one end; or a side may be broken into sections by walkways or doorways; or an island may be added to the basic plan. In farmhouse- or restaurant-style kitchens so large that the corners of a single work triangle would be too far apart *(far right),* several independent triangles may be designed instead — either with matching facilities to serve two or more cooks, or with special appliances or fixtures for tasks such as baking and canning.

In addition to providing an efficient work triangle, the floor plan should allow for a few other practical conventions of kitchen design. The sink is usually placed directly beneath a window, since the cook spends most time there; a stove at a window will spatter the glass with grease and might ignite curtains. The corners are especially tricky: To prevent cooks from bumping into each other at a corner, add 12 inches to the counter space recommended on pages 15-17 for each work center, measuring from the point where the front edges of the counters meet. Locate large appliances such as dishwashers and ovens at least 3 feet — preferably 4 feet or more — from a corner, so that their open horizontal doors cannot block access to base cabinets or strike a cook working at the corner.

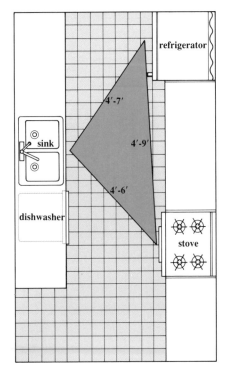

The galley kitchen. Best suited to a traffic-free cul-de-sac, the galley ideally should have walls 8 feet apart, leaving a 4-foot-wide corridor between the base cabinets; a 3-foot corridor is the practical minimum. Here, as in other triangles, the dishwasher may be to the left or the right of the sink; its placement is a matter of personal taste. The galley's storage capacity often is augmented with a pantry at the dead end.

The L kitchen. In a relatively square room this layout places the sink, stove or refrigerator at a right angle to the other two, or places two at right angles and puts the third in the corner between them as shown here. Either arrangement creates an efficient work triangle near the corner, out of the way of traffic. A diagonal-faced corner cabinet furnishes the most accessible corner storage.

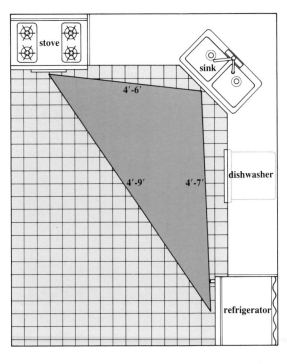

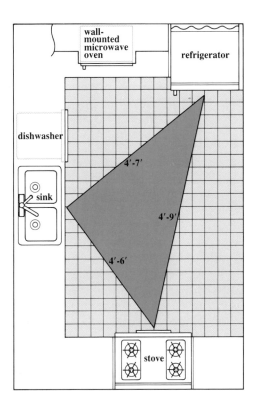

The U kitchen. By placing the sink, stove and refrigerator on three adjoining walls, this configuration expands countertop area and cabinet storage while creating a compact work triangle. For sufficient floor space, the base cabinets of the U's sides should be at least 5 feet apart. A microwave oven, standard in many kitchens, is most convenient for defrosting frozen foods or heating leftovers if placed beside the refrigerator.

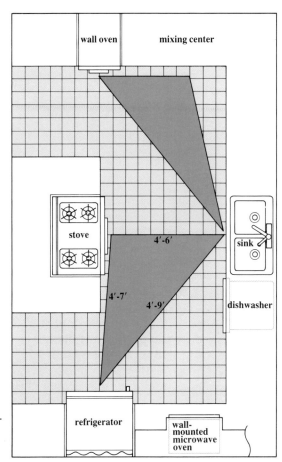

Adding extra triangles. This basic U-shaped plan, supplemented by an island, has two work triangles: A standard triangle between the refrigerator, the stove and the sink alongside a special baking-area triangle between the sink, a mixing center and a wall oven. Because extra triangles have various purposes and equipment, their sides may vary in length from 4 to 9 feet, as long as the resulting area is compact and efficient.

Tactics for Major Remodeling

The projects on the following pages can enhance any kitchen's appearance and function, but they cannot overcome all the inherent problems of an inefficient work triangle, cramped space or antiquated appliances. In such situations the only cure is major surgery — tearing out old cabinets and appliances, sometimes even walls, and installing new ones in different places.

Few homeowners tackle such tasks alone. Extensive renovation demands the diverse skills of a half dozen specialists. But as you direct them, this book can help you build a better kitchen — and save money.

For the design, you would be wise to collaborate with an architect or a specialist in kitchen design. At the least, hire a professional for a few hours of advice and pay for the drafting work to translate your sketches into blueprints.

The only rigid constraint on your plans is the building code. Plumbing, electrical and building inspectors all will have to approve your plans before remodeling begins, and then they must check the work itself. Although local codes vary considerably, here are some rules of thumb:

● Before demolishing a wall, consult an architect or engineer. Walls that do not support the house's framework generally can be removed easily; bearing walls can be altered only at great expense.

● Old ½-inch water lines can be extended from a sink to a dishwasher and an icemaker, but plumbing drains are less changeable. Extensions of more than a foot or two require an expensive new network of vent pipes to route sewer gases out through the roof.

● The old electrical system often must be upgraded. Most codes now require two 20-ampere small-appliance circuits in the kitchen and the dining room, with at least one grounded (three-pronged) receptacle over every counter.

● An old stove's electric or gas supply line is easy to extend, but an exhaust hood requires a short, concealed duct route to an exterior vent.

When taking bids for the job, you may want to stipulate that you will do some straightforward work — anything from painting *(pages 102-107)* to installing new cabinets *(pages 64-77)*. If you have enough time, you even can dispense with a contractor and coordinate the many specialty workers yourself.

In either case, you should arrange to stay at home throughout the project to solve the inevitable series of unanticipated (and unbudgeted) problems, each of which requires a quick solution. In these predicaments, try to change your original plan as little as possible: Any change will usually spawn other revisions in cabinet sizes, appliance specifications and the like, delaying the work and adding many dollars to its cost.

Put all of your instructions in writing, to forestall misunderstandings. And remember that construction schedules are notoriously unreliable; plan to cook on a hot plate and to eat from paper plates for roughly twice the promised interval. A custom-built kitchen is worth the wait.

Dressing up old cabinets

For most kitchens, the cabinets that are there already will do nicely. About all they are likely to need is a little cosmetic to improve their appearance or a minor refurbishing with storage organizers such as the sampling shown below.

Beautification generally comes first, because cabinets are the dominant element of the kitchen and establish its style. Changing their color with a coat of paint — and, perhaps, jaunty stripes — can bring a fresh aspect to the entire room (*pages 22-24*). Stripping off existing paint from wood cabinets so they can be stained and varnished (*page 25*) is another tack to take, and a particularly apt one if your aim is to produce a kitchen with a rustic look.

More subtle, but equally rewarding, effects are to be achieved with woodwork and hardware. Fitting strips of wood molding together in geometric shapes, for example,

forms classic ornaments for cabinet doors or drawers or both (*pages 28-29*). Affixing new knobs or handles of whatever type you fancy is even easier (*pages 26-27*). And fastening fluorescent lamps to the undersides of cabinets, though not decorating in the strictest sense of the word, makes the room a brighter place to work.

Improving on cabinet interiors realizes many goals. New racks, partitions, shelves and trays will help you arrange food and gear in the tidiest possible order, thus expanding the usable capacity of cabinets so you can store more items at appropriate work centers and thereby reduce the number of steps you need to take for any given chore. The wood shelves on pages 30-31, for instance, can be tailored to fit on the backs of the doors of the cabinets at your mixing center and can then display your choice of spices and the like. The simple wood drawer rack on page

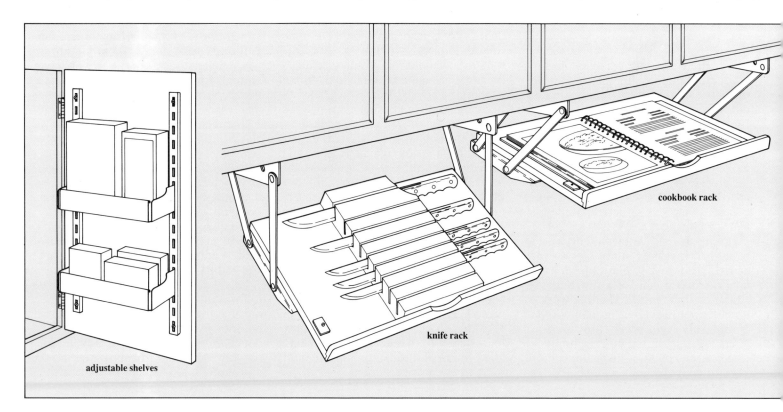

adjustable shelves

knife rack

cookbook rack

32 will bring order to an assortment of small jars and bottles while keeping their labels visible.

In addition to storage devices you may contrive, you can pick and choose from the array of ready-made fittings sold at lumberyards and home centers, at houseware, hardware and kitchen-supply stores. The ubiquitous drawer dividers of plastic for cutlery and wood for knives need only be set in place. Gadgets for the back of a cabinet door — stainless-steel or vinyl-coated-wire holders for bags, trays for detergents and dispensers for paper towels — are simply anchored with a few screws. Driving screws into a cabinet without splitting the wood or particleboard requires having holes drilled almost — but not quite — as deep as the screws are long. To ensure against drilling through the door, wrap adhesive tape around the shaft of the drill bit to indicate the required depth for the hole.

The stainless-steel brackets for the adjustable shelves at bottom left are also screwed to the door back. Scaled for cabinets, they are 19½ inches high. The enameled metal shelves they support are boxlike to keep the contents safe when the door swings. The shelves are 2 inches high, 4 inches deep and come in widths of 8, 12 and 18 inches.

Both the wood knife rack and cookbook holder opposite, near left, attach to the bottom of a wall cabinet. They pull down and forward into full view when needed, but otherwise fold back out of sight behind the front lip of the cabinet. Since both devices are held with screws, the cabinet bottom must be at least ⅜ inch thick to have the screws grip tight without poking up through it.

More sophisticated fittings such as the glide-out units below, left and center can provide the efficiency of fancy custom cabinets at a relatively low cost. The glides consist of paired channels: a fixed channel screwed to a base-cabinet wall or floor and — within it — a sliding channel attached to a drawer, tray or basket. Ball bearings and nylon rollers make the sliding almost effortless. The wood-front drawers and coated-wire baskets shown come in widths from 11½ to 21 inches; the top basket of the under-sink unit can be set on either side to avoid sink pipes.

Installing glide-out units demands clearing the base cabinet. Shelves often can be merely lifted out or unscrewed from their supports; supports should be unscrewed, then tapped with a hammer to break their glue bond and release them. A shelf that is glued into interlocking joints at its sides must be cut free, a section at a time, with a saber saw. Start by sawing a V-shaped cut from the front to the back of the shelf, then work toward the sides. Tap the last pieces with a hammer until you can jiggle them free.

The revolving shelf unit also requires a cleared cabinet. Its enameled metal shelves — in diameters from 18 to 28 inches — revolve around a matching post to create a lazy susan for small containers. For shelves that will revolve smoothly, the post must be absolutely vertical. To effect this, mark the location for the top bracket inside the roof of the cabinet, and use a plumb bob (page 122) to position the bottom bracket. At that stage, it is simple to assemble the shelves and post and adjust their height before fitting the post in place and putting the shelves to work.

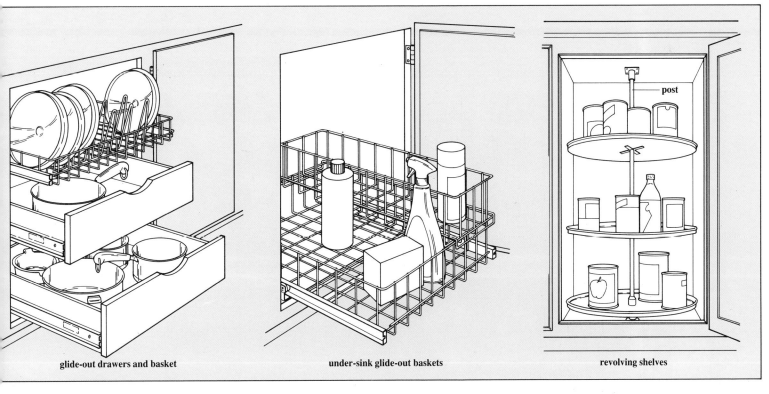

glide-out drawers and basket   under-sink glide-out baskets   revolving shelves

Paint: A freshening finish

Whether the color you want for your cabinets is light or dark, subtle or assertive, alkyd and latex paints provide it in a form that is quick and easy to apply. Both brush on smoothly. Latexes dry within two hours, alkyds overnight. In both, high-gloss paint has the highest resin content and thus the hardest surface. For durability, however, an alkyd is preferable: It forms a continuous film, whereas a latex film is microporous, permitting stains and moisture to penetrate.

Paint will bond to nearly any previous coating, with a few stipulations. Plastic-faced cabinets must be tested: Wipe a small, hidden area with paint thinner, apply alkyd primer, let it dry, and brush on alkyd paint; if the test patch dries without

wrinkling, the entire cabinet can be painted similarly. When painting over a dark color with a lighter one, you may need two or three coats for adequate coverage.

A neat paint job takes preparation. Clean the previous finish, then roughen it; painters call this "cutting a tooth." The quickest way is to use an orbital sander for large areas (Step 3) and a narrow strip of doubled sandpaper in hard-to-reach spots. Or you can do the entire job by hand, using a ready-made sandpaper holder or sandpaper wrapped around a scrap of 1-by-3. Remove sanding dust with a brush or a vacuum cleaner.

Once walls and floors are protected by dropcloths, newspaper and masking tape, the brushwork can begin. It goes most easily with tools tailored to each part of

the job, although a smaller brush can substitute for a larger one. A 3-inch wall brush is ideal for broad flat surfaces, a 2-inch trim brush for cabinet fronts and doorframes, a 1-inch trim brush for narrow edges, a foam-tipped applicator for irregular surfaces. Natural-bristled brushes are customarily used with alkyd paint, less expensive nylon-bristled brushes with latex.

When the job is done, wash brushes with several changes of clean solvent — water for latex, paint thinner or turpentine (a stronger but smellier solvent) for alkyd. Being flammable, alkyd solvents require good ventilation and special handling; dirty solvent should be sealed in a can and disposed of at a gas station, never dumped into sinks or storm drains.

1 **Taking off hardware.** Open one door at a time. Pressing firmly on the knob or handle with one hand, use a screwdriver to remove the screw and washer from the inside of the door or drawer front. Set the hardware aside, together with the drawers and any movable shelves. Label the inside of each drawer to indicate its position.

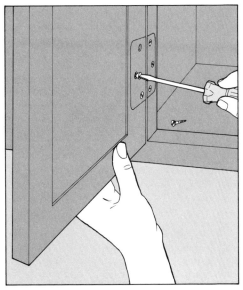

2 **Removing the doors.** Support a door with one hand and unscrew all of the hinge leaves that are visible when the door is closed. If both leaves are concealed, unfasten whichever is easiest to reach. When all of the doors are freed, use masking tape to cover the hinge leaves you left screwed onto the door or the cabinet frame. Set the doors aside in proper sequence, to ensure a good match when reinstalling them.

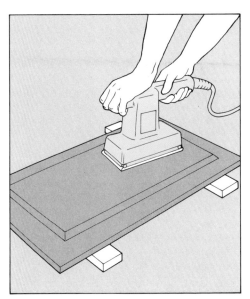

3 **Preparing the surfaces.** Sponge the cabinets with a solution of ¼ cup of ammonia in 1 gallon of water and rinse them with water. After the cabinets dry, fit an orbital sander with fine (150-grit) sandpaper. Wearing goggles and a dust mask, slide the sander across all surfaces in long, steady strokes, in the direction of the wood's grain if it is visible. Sand edges and corners by hand with folded sandpaper. Dust well.

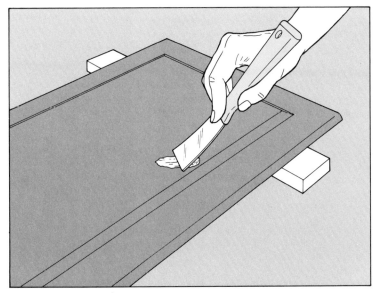

4 **Repairing damage.** To fill gouges, press wood putty into each depression with a flexible-bladed putty knife, then scrape the knife edge across the surface to level the patch. Let the putty dry overnight; sand lightly, feathering the edges. Dust thoroughly. Most scratches require only sanding, which blends the depression imperceptibly into the surface.

5 **Painting the cabinet.** Dip the bottom third of a 3-inch wall brush in paint; tap the brush against the paint can to shake off any excess. Starting at the top of the back wall of each cabinet, paint a 1-foot-square section with even, parallel strokes. Then brush overlapping sections beside and below it; always paint from a bare area toward wet paint.

Working from the top down, paint the side walls, the cabinet ceiling, both sides of each permanent shelf and the floor; use a 1-inch trim brush for narrow edges. Finally, paint the cabinet's exterior — the sides, the front and (on a wall cabinet) the bottom.

TIP: Be sure to stir the paint frequently with a wooden paddle to keep the pigments distributed evenly as you work. ▶

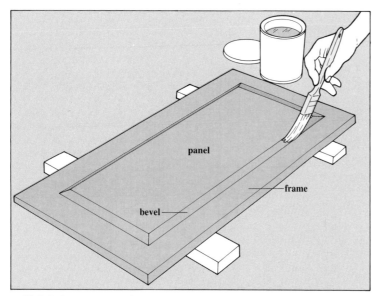

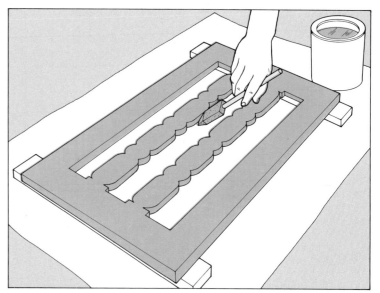

6 **Painting the doors.** Place each door face down on wood scraps, paint its back and edges, and let the paint dry overnight; then turn the door over and paint the face. Treat the shelves similarly. On a frame-and-panel door *(above)*, paint each side in stages: Paint the outer frame with a 2-inch brush, the panel's face with a 3-inch brush and finally the panel's beveled edges with light strokes of a 1-inch brush; take particular care to avoid paint build-up beside the bevel.

Paint the face and interior of each drawer; leave the sides of the drawer and the cabinet's matching glides unpainted to prevent sticking.

7 **Painting intricate edges.** Paint the edges of a fancy cutout pattern *(above)* or a geometrical relief with a foam-tipped applicator designed to reach into tight spots and to spread paint over uneven surfaces. Handle the foam-tipped applicator just as you would an ordinary brush: Dip it in paint, allow a few moments for the paint to seep through the foam, shake off the excess and gently stroke the foam tip across the wood.

Let the paint dry until the surfaces are no longer sticky. Then replace the hardware and hinges, and slide in the shelves and drawers.

Painting Perfect Stripes

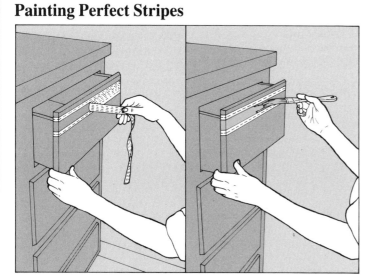

Sharp-edged accents. For stripes on cabinets, apply the special scored masking tape designed for putting racing stripes on cars and available where automobile supplies are sold. Draw the line for positioning the top edge of the tape ¼ inch higher than you want that edge of the stripe to be; using a carpenter's level will ensure a perfectly horizontal line. Press the tape carefully into place, cut off the end, then tear away enough ¹⁄₁₆-inch-wide strips to expose a band of the desired width *(above, left)*. Lightly sand the exposed surface, then dust it. Press the tape tight once again, then paint the stripe *(above, right)*; after the paint has dried, you can peel away the tape and erase the pencil line.

Stain and varnish to enhance wood's grain

Many old cabinets can contribute a glowing richness to a kitchen if they are simply stripped of paint and given a natural finish. Solid wood cabinets are always good candidates for such treatment. Plywood cabinets, however, vary in their suitability: Beneath their old paint finish may lie anything from a handsome oak veneer to much-patched birch; test one door and, if need be, repaint it. Cabinets with plastic or particleboard faces cannot qualify, of course.

Before stripping a cabinet, remove the doors and drawers, unscrew all hardware, immerse any painted hardware in paint remover (afterward, lacquer it to prevent tarnishing), and protect the surrounding area with dropcloths and masking tape. Use a nonflammable, paste-type paint remover in a well-ventilated room and follow the instructions carefully. To eliminate discolorations, bleach the wood. Then patch any damage, sand the exterior, and dust it.

Finish the cabinet in two steps: First apply an oil-based stain to even the wood color. Then brush on three coats of polyurethane varnish, a durable clear coating available in glossy and satin versions.

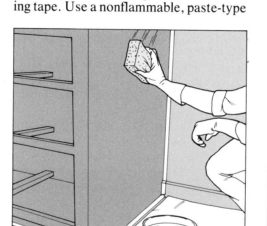

1 **Stripping old paint.** Wearing goggles and rubber gloves, use a cheap nylon-bristled paintbrush to apply a thick coat of paste-type paint remover to a 2-foot-square area. Leave the remover undisturbed until the paint forms bubbles (15 to 30 minutes). Gently scrape away the resulting sludge with a putty knife or a paint scraper, wiping the tool clean on newspaper. If necessary, repeat this process until you reach bare wood, then strip subsequent sections.

2 **Bleaching.** Wearing goggles and gloves, wash the cabinet with steel wool dipped in the solvent recommended for your paint remover. Let the wood dry. Dip a sponge in commercial wood bleach or in laundry bleach, and rub the bleach into one face of the cabinet. Wait two minutes, then sponge away the bleach with lots of warm water. Repeat this process until all of the stains have disappeared, then bleach the other cabinets to match the first one.

3 **Staining.** Sand and dust or vacuum the cabinet, then use a folded rag to rapidly apply a thin coat of oil-based stain to one face; wait 30 seconds, then quickly wipe off the stain with a clean rag. For a darker color, stain the wood repeatedly, counting the applications. Apply stain identically to all exterior faces, to both sides of the doors, and to the drawer fronts. Then rub the entire cabinet to even the color; allow the stain to dry for 24 hours.

4 **Varnishing.** Sand and dust the stained surfaces. Dip the bristles of a paintbrush halfway into polyurethane varnish, tap the brush against the can and make one long vertical stroke on the cabinet, then dip the brush again. Start each new stroke at the edge of the last one; overlapping strokes will cause bubbles. Let the varnish dry overnight; sand lightly with extra-fine (200- to 400-grit) paper, and dust again. Apply two more coats.

New hardware: A change of accents

Cabinet hardware — whether polished brass, Art Deco chrome or the porcelain-and-brass knobs shown below — is a sort of architectural grace note, an easy-to-change ornament that imparts distinction to the entire kitchen.

Knobs and handles for doors and drawers sometimes can be replaced simply by fitting the screws for the new hardware through the old holes, but often you must drill new holes instead — a task that also lets you adjust the hardware's placement to your convenience and taste. The job is easiest when done in conjunction with repainting the cabinets *(pages 22-24),* because the old holes, once filled with wood putty, become invisible beneath the new coat of paint; otherwise, the filled and sanded holes require touch-up painting.

The primary consideration in placing knobs and handles is symmetry, so that the kitchen's various parts all have the same pleasing proportions. You can achieve consistent placement by measuring each door or drawer and marking its face with light pencil lines, which you can later erase. But if you have more than half a dozen or so handles to install, measuring for each one will become tedious, and you are likely to make mistakes. You can vastly simplify the task of locating handles with two plywood jigs — homemade drilling guides that will align the holes identically on each door and drawer.

Doorknobs and handles ordinarily are installed 1 to 2 inches from each door's unhinged edge. The distances from the bottom of the door on a wall cabinet and from the top of the door on a base cabinet can be identical or not, as you like.

If the distances match, one jig can be flipped over sidewise or lengthwise to automatically position every door handle. If not, you will need separate jigs for the handles on the wall and base cabinets.

Handles for doors can be located and attached with the doors hung in place. By contrast, the measuring, marking and installing of handles for drawers requires emptying and removing them.

Typically, a single drawer pull is centered on the drawer; pairs of pulls are equidistant from the sides of the drawer face. Either way, the pulls are placed at or slightly above the drawer's vertical center, but always at the same distance below the top of each drawer; this scheme ensures that the handles on drawers of varying heights will remain aligned.

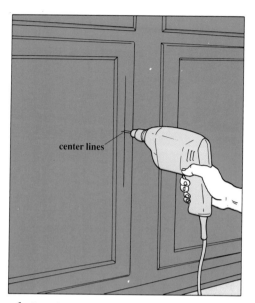

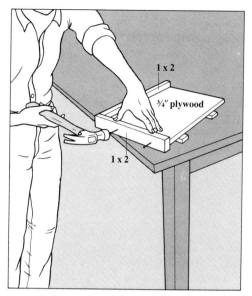

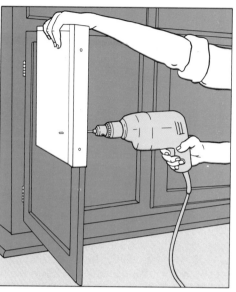

1 **Locating a door handle.** With the door shut, pencil a vertical line about an inch from the door's unhinged edge. Hold the handle centered on the line at a comfortable height, and mark the door at the center of each screw hole. At each mark, drill a hole of the same diameter as the machine screws that fasten the handle. Keep the drill bit exactly perpendicular to the door's face.

2 **Making a door-handle jig.** Cut a scrap of ¾-inch plywood about one foot square. Center strips of 1-by-2 along two adjacent edges of the plywood and fasten them with fourpenny nails. Here, the strips are about a foot long, but shorter lengths would serve.

3 **Drilling the jig.** Open the door, and place the jig against its outside face. Align the jig behind the drilled corner by resting the strips against the door's edges. Hold the plywood tightly, then slide your drill bit through the holes made in Step 1, and drill matching ones in the jig. Align the jig similarly at the other doors, then drill them through its holes and install the handles.

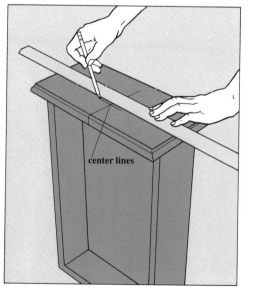

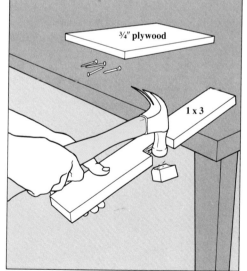

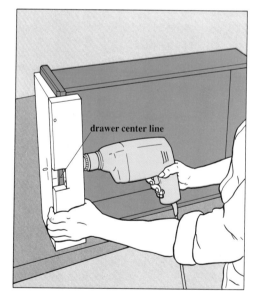

4 **Locating a single drawer handle.** Remove a typical drawer and stand it upright. Mark the center of each drawer edge, then draw short intersecting center lines on the drawer face between the marks. Center the handle on the vertical line, and position its holes on or slightly above the horizontal one. Mark and drill the holes as you did in Step 1.

5 **Fashioning a drawer-handle jig.** Cut a plywood rectangle nearly as wide as the drawer's height and about 10 inches long, then cut a 1-by-3 the same length. Mark the center of the 1-by-3. With a crosscut saw *(page 122)*, make two parallel cuts, each 1 inch from center and 1¼ inches deep. Strike the block of wood between the cuts sharply with a hammer *(above)*, knocking it out, and fasten the strip perpendicular to the plywood's edge, using fourpenny nails.

6 **Using the jig.** Measure along the strip, and mark a center line across the plywood edge, within the notch made in Step 5. Hold the plywood against the drawer face, and rest the strip on the drawer's top edge; then align the center lines for the drawer and jig, and drill the jig through the drawer's holes *(above)*. Pencil a tiny center line on the top edge of each subsequent drawer; align the jig with the line, drill through the jig into the drawer and install the handles.

Decorative molding for doors and drawers

Plain wood cabinets can take on an air of elegance if moldings are added. With the wide variety of moldings available, you can evoke almost any style, from Colonial American to French Provincial.

Moldings with smooth profiles are most suitable for kitchens. Ornate, embossed moldings collect grease and dust in their grooves and are difficult to clean.

In the example shown at far right, simple rectangles of molding add distinction to cabinet doors. The same shape could enhance drawers, or you could experiment on either drawers or doors with octagons, diamonds or combinations of geometric forms. As a first step, plot your design on graph paper, then cut full-sized paper models. Tape them in place to see if they please you.

Lumberyards sell kits of molding already cut to standard cabinet sizes, but it is considerably cheaper to buy molding by the foot and produce your own designs. With a backsaw and miter box, you can easily make both 45° cuts for mitered joints and 90° cuts for butt joints. The backsaw's thick steel blade is held straight by a rigid spine, and the paired slots in the miter box keep its cutting edge on track. Before using a new miter box, extend the slots by sawing through the sides until you reach the box's floor.

To determine the amount of molding you need, first measure the perimeter of each pattern and multiply by the number of times that pattern will be applied. Then add 20 per cent to allow for the unusable offcuts from standard molding lengths.

Templates made of picture-mounting mat board — shown here — or of firm cardboard are used in cutting and assembling the molding pieces and in fixing them to the cabinets. A template made to fit the largest cabinet doors often can be reduced later to fit smaller doors: Simply cut across the middle of each side, overlap the pieces to conform to the smaller size, and tape the template back together.

To assemble the molding, you will need ¾-inch finishing nails, a nail set, a hammer and carpenter's wood glue. You can paint or varnish the molding (pages 22-25) before fixing it to the doors, and later touch up the putty-filled nail holes with a small brush. If, instead, you paint the molding after it is in place, protect the finish of the cabinet with masking tape along the molding edges.

1 **Cutting the template.** Remove the cabinet doors (page 23, Steps 1-2), drawers and any protruding hardware. Lay the largest cabinet door on a sheet of mat board and trace the door's outline. Using a carpenter's square as a straightedge, cut along the lines with a utility knife; draw the knife toward you to make the cuts. Next, measure and mark lines for the outer edges of the molding rectangle you wish to form on the mat board, making sure your molding will not interfere with the door's hardware. Keep the lines for the molding parallel to the mat board's edges and make the width of the margins even. Then use the carpenter's square and utility knife to cut along the lines of the template (above).

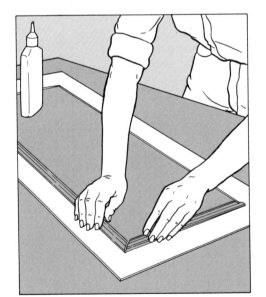

5 **Assembling the rectangle.** Fit all four pieces into the template to make sure the mitered ends form neat joints. Take out the pieces, apply a thin film of carpenter's glue to both ends of each piece, and fit the pieces into the template again. Wait 30 minutes for the glue to dry. Caution: Do not wipe off excess glue, lest you smudge it; you can chip it off with a knife after it dries.

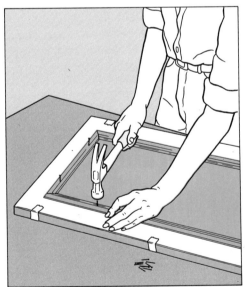

6 **Attaching the molding to a door.** Tap ¾-inch finishing nails into the molding an inch from each corner, driving them in until they stand by themselves. Tape the template to the door, aligning the edges precisely. Coat the underside of the molding thinly with glue. Then press the rectangle into the template and against the door. While the glue is wet, drive in the nails, leaving their heads about ⅛ inch above the surface (above). Remove the template.

2 **Cutting the first angle.** Place a strip of molding on its flat back in a miter box, with the edge that will become the outside edge of your rectangle against the far side of the box. Position the strip so its end is just beyond the 45° guide slot at your left. If the strip reaches beyond the worktable, support the free end so the strip does not break under its own weight. Hold the molding in place, slip the saw into the guides *(above)* and cut the angle.

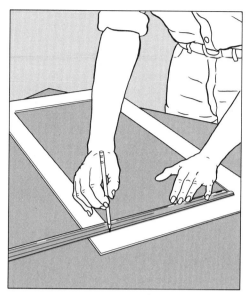

3 **Marking for the next cut.** Fit the angled end of the molding strip into a corner of the template and push the molding's outside edge against the template's inner edge. Then mark the outside edge of the strip for the next corner cut *(above)*.

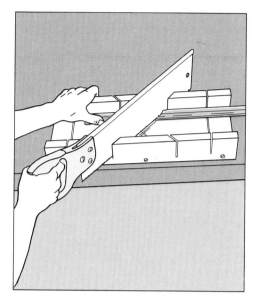

4 **Mitering the next corner.** Put the strip against the far side of the miter box, with the already-sawed angle to your left and the new cutting mark in front of the guide slot on your right. Saw the new corner angle.

Using the template to determine the position and angle of each cut, saw the remaining pieces of your molding rectangle. Smooth off any ragged edges on the sawed ends with fine (150-grit) sandpaper.

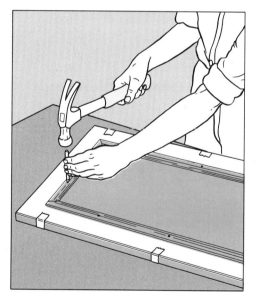

7 **Countersinking the nails.** Place the recessed tip of a nail set over the head of a nail. Tap the nail set until the nailhead is driven 1/16 inch below the molding surface. After setting all the nails, fill the holes with wood putty. Complete all the doors of one size, then reduce the dimensions of the template — or make a new one — and proceed to smaller doors or drawers. Let the putty dry for at least 4 hours, then sand it smooth.

Spice racks on a door

Although savory spices are a cook's delight, their containers rank high on the list of life's little nuisances. Without special storage, spice jars or cans inevitably become jumbled with other foods, frustrating the cook and wasting shelf space; and unless the containers are set in rows, their labels prove hard to read. The racks pictured at left — built with only a miter box (text, page 28), a backsaw, a hammer and a power drill — solve these problems. Fastened to the inside of a cabinet door, the racks keep the spice containers neat and easily accessible.

The racks can be hung on any sturdy door that is at least ⅜ inch thick. They tuck between the shelves, extending less than 3 inches into the cabinet, so they do not significantly diminish its expected storage capacity.

The 15-inch-long rack described here will fit neatly into most wall or base cabinets, but the dimensions can easily be tailored to particular situations. If the doors of your cabinets have frame-and-panel construction, simply match the rack's length to the width of the inner panel; for a plain door, allow 1 inch of clearance at each end of the rack.

The racks can be finished either with paint (pages 22-24) or — as at left — with stain and varnish (page 25).

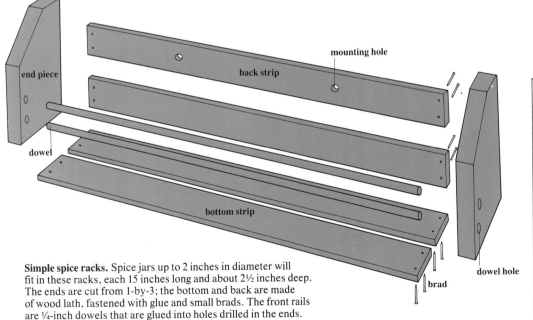

Simple spice racks. Spice jars up to 2 inches in diameter will fit in these racks, each 15 inches long and about 2½ inches deep. The ends are cut from 1-by-3; the bottom and back are made of wood lath, fastened with glue and small brads. The front rails are ¼-inch dowels that are glued into holes drilled in the ends.

Materials List (for one rack)	
1 x 3	1 clear pine 1 x 3, 10″ long, cut into 2 pieces, 5″ long
Lath	1 piece ¼″ x 1⅜″ wood lath, 5′ long, cut into 4 strips, 15″ long
Dowel	1 ¼″ wood dowel, 3′ long, cut into 2 pieces, 15″ long
Screws	2 No. 6 oval-head wood screws, ⅝″ long
Brads	about 16 brads, ¾″ long
Stain	oil-based wood stain
Varnish	polyurethane varnish

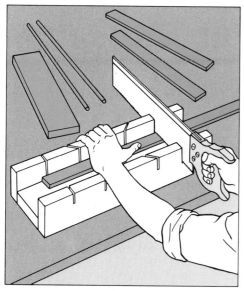

1 **Cutting lath and dowels.** Using a backsaw and a miter box, cut four 15-inch pieces of unblemished lath and two matching lengths of ¼-inch dowel: Set the backsaw in the miter box's right-angled slots and, for each piece in turn, align the waste side of your pencil line with one side of the saw blade. Hold the wood tightly against the back of the miter box with one hand, and saw through it with light, smooth strokes.

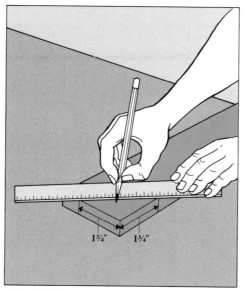

2 **Making the ends.** Using the miter box, cut a 10-inch length of 1-by-3, then mark both an end and an edge 1¾ inches from the same corner and draw a line between the marks. Set the backsaw in the miter box's 45° slots, place the pencil line just outside the blade, and saw along the line. Bevel the other end, then cut the board squarely midway between the beveled ends.

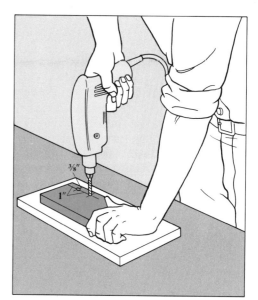

3 **Drilling the dowel holes.** On the face of each 1-by-3, draw a line ⅜ inch from the short edge. Mark the line 1 and 2 inches from the 1-by-3's square end. Hold the board down very firmly on scrap wood and, at each mark, slowly drill a ¼-inch hole exactly perpendicular to the board's face.

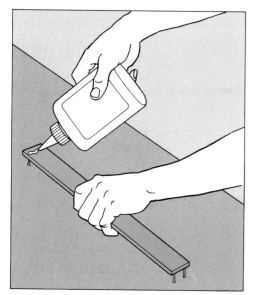

4 **Assembling the back.** About ⅜ inch from each end of one piece of lath, tap down two ¾-inch brads until their tips emerge on the other side. Then squeeze a thin bead of glue across the tips. Nail the lath to the long edge of each 1-by-3, flush with its square bottom. Glue and nail a second lath into place 1⅜ inches above the first.

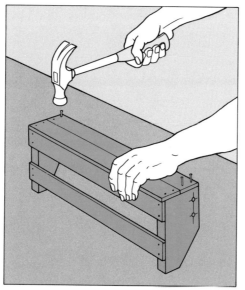

5 **Adding the bottom.** Start brads in the remaining two pieces of lath, and run a thin line of glue across each end as in Step 4. Place the rack beveled end down, and use brads to secure each lath to the square bottoms of the end pieces, one flush with the lath back, the other with the front of the 1-by-3s.

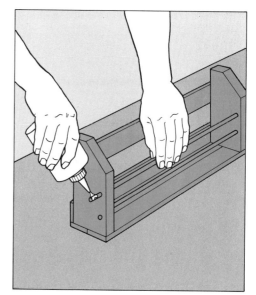

6 **Gluing the dowels.** Test the fit of the two dowels by sliding them into place through the holes in the 1-by-3s; if a dowel binds, sand it down. Pull the dowels back slightly and smear glue on their ends, then push and twist the dowels until the ends are flush with the outer faces of the 1-by-3s; wipe away excess glue. Drill two holes in the center of the back's upper lath, 3 inches from each end. Mount the rack on the door, using ⅝-inch oval-head wood screws.

A spice rack in a drawer

Where spice jars can be stored handily in a drawer near the stove, the rack at right offers an ingenious and economical method. Consisting only of a plywood base and quarter-round dividers, the rack prevents jars from rolling and tilts their tops upward for easy access.

The drawer ought to be a minimum of 3½ inches deep to accommodate the combined height of ⅜-inch plywood, ¾-inch quarter-round molding and spice jars approximately 2 inches in diameter. Should the drawer be larger than you need it to be, you can build a rack that extends only partway into the drawer, leaving the rear free for seldom-used utensils and supplies. In this case, anchor the rack with finishing nails.

Space the dividers at intervals slightly greater than the height of your spice jars: In the steps below, the quarter-round dividers are set 4½ inches apart to support 4¼-inch-high spice jars. Once built, the rack can be finished with paint *(pages 22-24)* or stain and varnish *(page 25)*.

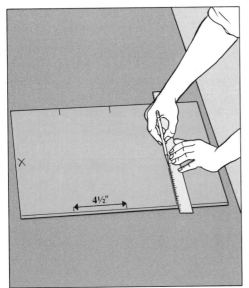

1 **Laying out the rack.** With a circular saw *(page 24)*, cut a piece of ⅜-inch plywood — in this case, birch-veneer plywood is used — ⅛ inch smaller in length and width than the bottom of the drawer. Alternatively, have a lumberyard cut the wood for you. Mark the front end of the plywood with an *X*. Then measure from the front along the sides with a ruler or a carpenter's square, and draw parallel lines every 4½ inches across the face of the wood.

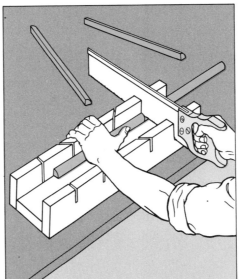

2 **Cutting the dividers.** Use a backsaw and a miter box to squarely cut ¾-inch quarter-round molding into pieces that match the width of the plywood sheet. Start ¾-inch brads in each piece at 5-inch intervals, driving the brads straight down into the molding's round side, parallel to one of the flat edges, until the brad tips barely protrude from the other flat edge.

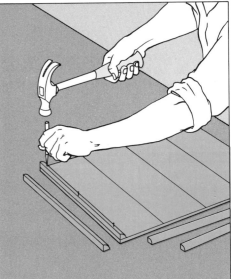

3 **Nailing the dividers.** Squeeze a thin line of glue between the protruding brad tips on a piece of the molding; set the molding's right-angled edge against the front of the plywood, with the round side of the molding facing the back. Hammer in the brads until their heads are barely ⅛ inch above the molding, then use a nail set *(above)* to drive the heads 1/16 inch below the surface. Nail the other dividers into place similarly and fill the nail holes with putty.

Concealed lighting for counters

The undersides of wall-mounted cabinets can house a solution to the irksome kitchen problem of poorly lit counters. Unobtrusive fluorescent fixtures, mounted individually or fastened in tandem along an entire run of cabinets, will shed abundant light on counter space.

Such lights are available at hardware stores or at retailers listed under "Lighting Fixtures" in the yellow pages of the telephone book. The simplest kinds come completely assembled and ready to hang. The kind shown here has a few extra components and takes a few more minutes to install, but its features lend convenience and versatility. It has a movable switch that you position yourself, an extra outlet for countertop appliances, and internal wiring that will allow you to wire one or more additional fixtures to the original one so that a row of lights can be turned on and off with the flick of a single switch (box, page 35).

Fixtures of this kind often come without a factory-attached power cord—allowing you to specify to the dealer the length and placement of the cord you want installed. Order a grounded No. 16 cord without a plug, installed so that the cord will extend from the end of the fixture nearest a convenient wall outlet. Be sure the cord is long enough to follow an inconspicuous route—generally behind the front bottom edges of the cabinets—from the mounted fixture to the outlet. Buy a three-prong grounding plug, which you can attach yourself (page 34, Step 6) after you have installed the light and cord.

You can buy a light fixture that is anywhere from 12 to 48 inches long; most are about 1¼ inches deep. The fixtures are unobtrusive on any surface; if mounted on a recessed cabinet bottom, they will be all but invisible to an adult of average height or taller.

The tools required for installation are few: a power drill, a screwdriver, a hammer and a packet of insulated wire staples. Buy mounting screws if the fixture comes without them. Make sure they are no longer than the thickness of the cabinet bottom, their heads no wider than the mounting hole on the fixture. Here, ⅜-inch No. 6 wood screws are used. To strip the wires before fastening the plug to the cord, you will need a utility knife; wire cutters ease the job of stripping insulation from wires, but they are not necessary.

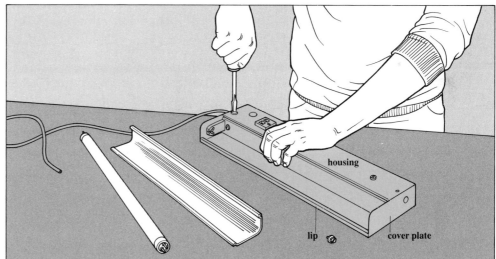

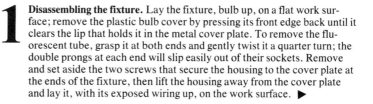

1 **Disassembling the fixture.** Lay the fixture, bulb up, on a flat work surface; remove the plastic bulb cover by pressing its front edge back until it clears the lip that holds it in the metal cover plate. To remove the fluorescent tube, grasp it at both ends and gently twist it a quarter turn; the double prongs at each end will slip easily out of their sockets. Remove and set aside the two screws that secure the housing to the cover plate at the ends of the fixture, then lift the housing away from the cover plate and lay it, with its exposed wiring up, on the work surface. ▶

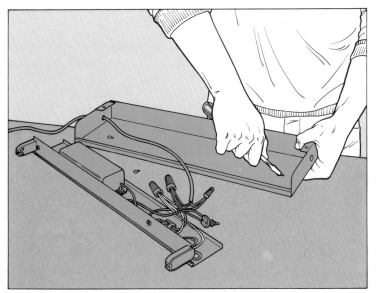

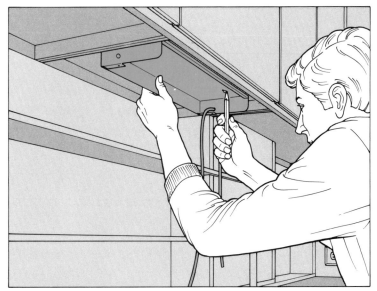

2 **Making two mounting holes.** Raise one end of the cover plate slightly off the work surface and, applying firm pressure with the tip of a screwdriver, bend the keyhole-shaped knockout away from its opening. If the metal tab does not pop out, twist it gently to pry it off. Remove the keyhole-shaped knockout at the other end of the cover plate.

3 **Mounting the cover plate.** Set the cover plate's roof against the bottom of the cabinet, and outline the keyhole-shaped mounting holes. Center the tip of the drill bit — here, a ⁵⁄₆₄-inch bit for a No. 6 wood screw — in the narrow part of each outline, and drill a ³⁄₈-inch hole. Twist the two mounting screws into the holes; leave each screwhead protruding ¹⁄₈ inch. Position the cover plate with the wide section of each mounting hole over its screw, then push the cover plate sideways so that the screws extend from the narrow portions of the holes. Tighten the screws.
TIP: To keep from drilling all the way through the cabinet bottom, wrap a piece of masking tape around the drill bit ³⁄₈ inch from the tip; stop drilling when the edge of the tape touches the wood.

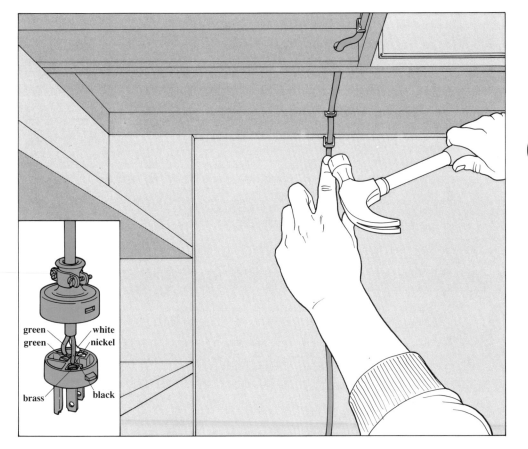

green
green
white
nickel
brass
black

6 **Anchoring the cord.** Starting near the fixture, drive an insulated wire staple to anchor the cord at the nearest convenient and inconspicuous spot — here, behind the bottom front edge of the cabinet overhang. At an obstacle such as adjacent bottom edges of the cabinet walls *(left),* drill a ³⁄₈-inch hole for the cord to pass through. When you reach the nearest convenient wall outlet, cut off all but 4 inches of the excess cord. Peel off the insulation and strip the wires, following the plug manufacturer's instructions; then connect the white wire to the nickel screw, the black wire to the brass screw and the green wire to the green screw *(inset).* Finally, replace the bulb and the bulb cover, and plug in the power cord.

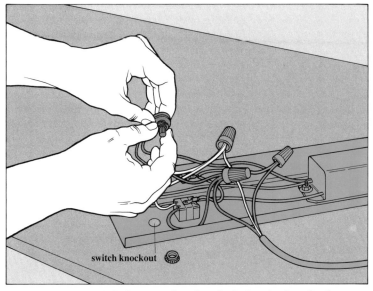

4 **Installing the switch.** Remove a knockout in the housing base for the fixture's switch. You may have several choices; pick the most convenient location, noting which side the switch will be on when you turn the housing over to install it. Twist the round washer and the nut off the threaded shaft of the switch *(above),* push the shaft of the switch down through its hole in the housing, and replace the nut and washer.

5 **Assembling the fixture.** Lift the housing into place against the cover plate, lining up the hole at each end of the housing with its corresponding hole on the small flange at either end of the cover plate *(above).* Be sure, as you push the housing into position, that no wires protrude around its edges. Twist the two screws removed in Step 1 into the aligned holes; turn each a few times with one hand as you hold the housing in place with the other, then tighten the screws with a screwdriver.

Wiring Lights in Tandem

If you wish to wire two or more fixtures together, you must buy units with internal wiring designed for this purpose; ask to have a power cord attached to each fixture so that it extends from the appropriate end.

For the two-unit installation below, you must splice the black, white and green wires from the power cord on the second, or auxiliary, unit to the corresponding wires in the housing of the primary unit. The primary unit is the one

that will have the working on-off switch.

For a chain of three or more fixtures, leave all but the primary unit's housing uninstalled and repeat the steps below for each pair of adjacent units, working toward the primary fixture.

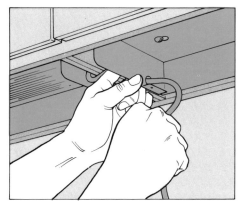

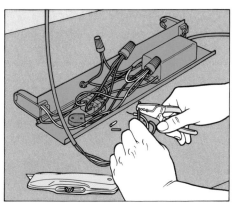

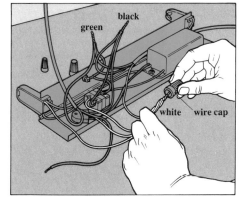

1 **Threading the power cord.** Install two fixtures, but leave the housing for the primary fixture on the counter. Remove a knockout in the primary unit's cover plate and pull the cord from the auxiliary fixture through the hole *(above);* leave slack so you can staple the cord to the cabinets later. Cut off all but about 18 inches of the cord with wire cutters or a utility knife.

2 **Stripping the wires.** Use a utility knife to cut a shallow 6-inch slit through the insulation at the end of the auxiliary cord; peel back and cut off the insulation. Then clamp the proper-sized notch of the wire cutters over each exposed inner wire 3/8 inch from the end; pull off the insulation. You can also strip the wires with a utility knife, but be careful not to cut any of their copper strands.

3 **Splicing.** Twist the wire caps counterclockwise off the black, white and green wires in the primary fixture's housing. To bind the ends of the wires with their corresponding wires from the auxiliary cord, twist each set of exposed strands clockwise together. Replace the wire caps, install the housing and anchor the power cord. Install a grounding plug *(Step 6, opposite).*

Crafting racks
and shelves

Kitchens seem to obey their own version of Parkinson's law: The number of items that must be kept somewhere expands to fill the space available. And if you have ever rummaged desperately through a utensil-cluttered drawer searching for the apple corer or the right-sized wire whisk, you know the problem is not simply space but orderly space: room to keep things organized and on view so you can find them easily.

Almost any kitchen can benefit from more shelves and racks for such utilitarian reasons. It also can profit esthetically. Cooking implements become vivid decorative accents when hung on a handsome rack. A shelf garden of aromatic herbs freshens the visual aspect of a kitchen. And shelves of bric-a-brac — antique bottles, perhaps, or a child's artistic triumphs in modeling clay — impart warmth to a room dominated by no-nonsense modern appliances.

Even a small, apparently crowded kitchen may have space for shelves or racks in unexpected places: above or across a window, at the back of a counter beneath wall cabinets, even hung from the ceiling. Where you position such open-storage units depends, of course, on what you plan to use them for. A magnetized knife holder should be within easy reach of your cutting surface; a rack for pots and pans belongs near your range *(pages 16-17)*.

Shops offer a variety of ready-made shelves and racks, and the stylistically adventurous can make surprising use of items never intended for the kitchen at all. A chain-link fence gate, for instance, with its metal frame and crisscross mesh of heavy-gauge wire, becomes a hi-tech rack when suspended horizontally from the ceiling by chains.

But if you want shelves and racks that are truly tailored to your needs and available space — and at less cost than virtually anything you might purchase — you can make them yourself. Kitchen open-storage units designed especially for this book are presented on pages 42-63, with illustrated step-by-step instructions to help you

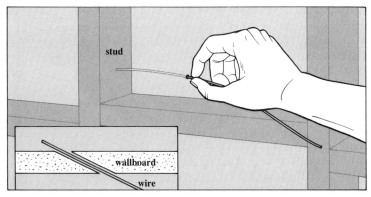

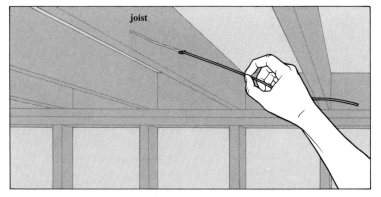

Finding a framing member. With your knuckles, tap lightly across the wallboard; a solid sound should reveal the approximate position of a wooden stud or ceiling joist. To locate a stud precisely, drill a small hole a few inches away and angled sharply *(inset, above, left)* toward the suspected location. Insert a thin, stiff wire until its tip meets the stud. (If you encounter cushiony resistance, the wire is probably running into insulation; try to push the tip on through.)

Grasp the wire at the hole with thumb and forefinger *(above, left)* to mark the distance from hole to timber. Then extract the wire, and position it at the same angle outside the wallboard. The wire's tip should now indicate the edge of the concealed stud; add ¾ inch to find the stud's center. Confirm the location by driving a nail through the wallboard until you feel it enter the wood.

Use the same process to locate a joist *(above, right)*. When drilling overhead, wear safety goggles to keep plaster dust out of your eyes.

To determine a point anywhere else along the center line of any timber you have located, measure an equivalent distance from an adjacent wall, then confirm by driving a nail.

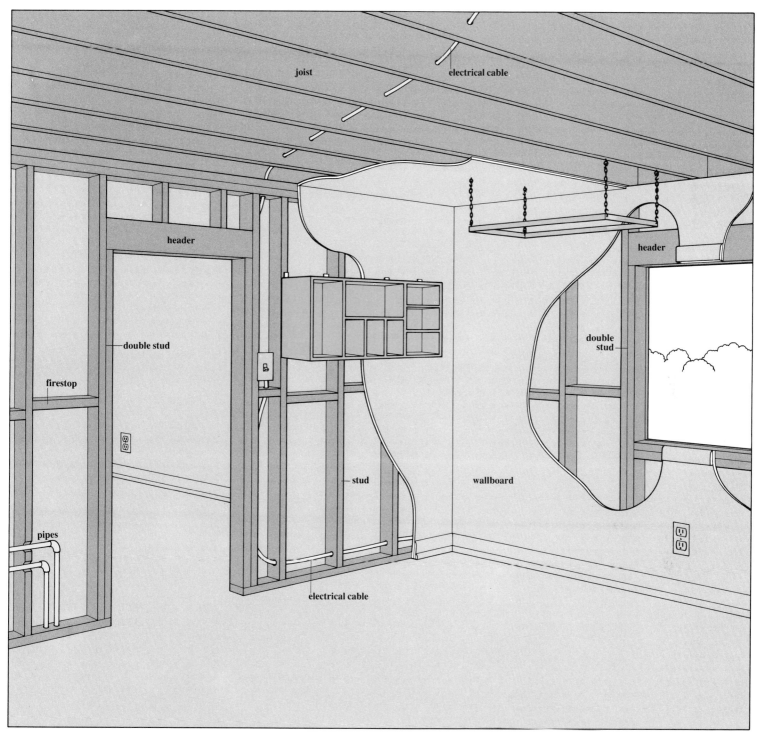

joist

electrical cable

header

double stud

firestop

pipes

stud

electrical cable

wallboard

double stud

header

Hidden anchorages for heavy loads. The wood framework of a modern house provides a wealth of firm holds for racks and shelves. Behind wallboard walls, 2-by-4 studs are spaced at 16-inch intervals — that is, 16 inches from the center of one stud to the center of the next. (In some houses, studs may be at wider intervals.)

Short 2-by-4s, called firestops, are placed horizontally between studs to retard upward flame movement in the event of a fire in a wall. Double studs alongside doors and windows, and timber assemblies called headers above those openings, offer additional gripping space for fasteners. Ceiling joists, 2-by-10s that normally span the narrower dimension of a structure, also are usually at 16-inch intervals.

When drilling holes, beware of pipes and cables. You can get some idea of their placement by looking for plumbing and electrical outlets, not only in the kitchen but in rooms above, below and adjoining it. Electric cable is most often attached to the sides of studs and joists or is run through transverse holes set at least 1½ inches from the faces of those framing members, beyond the reach of most pilot holes you might be drilling for fasteners. However, pipes are usually set in notches cut across the faces of studs. Unless your walls have metal studs (common in recently constructed apartment buildings), immediately cease drilling if you feel the drill bit strike metal.

This table indicates appropriate fasteners for loads of various weight and walls of different types. If you do not know the construction of your wall, drill a small hole where you wish to hang something, noting the resistance you meet and the dust that emerges. You may have to stop drilling and pull the bit out slowly to examine the dust on it. Then consult the column headed ''Test-hole clues.'' Next, divide the probable weight of your loaded shelf or rack by the number of fasteners you plan to use. The ''Light or medium load'' column suggests devices to hold loads up to 20 pounds per fastener. The ''Heavy load'' column is for items between 20 and 50 pounds for each fastener.

Fasteners to Fit the Job

WALL TYPE	TEST-HOLE CLUES	LIGHT OR MEDIUM LOAD	HEAVY LOAD
Wallboard or lath and plaster	White dust and little resistance as bit quickly breaks through (wallboard). White dust followed by brown dust; moderate resistance (plaster over lath).	Picture hook, or plastic anchor with matching wood screw (or self-tapping screw) for a very light load. For a medium load, Molly to match wall thickness or toggle bolt ¼″ in diameter.	Molly to match wall thickness, or toggle bolt ¼″ or greater in diameter. (Caution: Wallboard may crumble under heavy loads.)
Wallboard or plaster over wood stud	White dust only (wallboard) or white dust followed by brown dust (plaster over lath) before wood shavings appear. Increased resistance as wood shavings appear.	No. 6 to No. 8 wood screw long enough to penetrate at least 1″ into the wood stud.	No. 8 to No. 10 wood screw long enough to penetrate at least 1½″ into the wood stud. For a heavier load, lag bolt or hanger bolt at least ¼″ in diameter and long enough to reach at least 1½″ into the stud.
Wallboard or plaster over metal stud	White dust only (wallboard) or white dust followed by brown dust (plaster over lath) before metal shavings appear. Very heavy resistance as metal shavings appear.	Self-tapping sheet-metal screw, No. 6 or larger, long enough to reach about ½″ beyond the thin face of the metal stud.	Self-tapping sheet-metal screw, No. 8 or larger, long enough to reach about ½″ beyond the thin face of the metal stud.
Thick plaster	White dust. Steady moderate resistance. A bit less than 3″ long does not break through.	Expansion shield with machine screw ¼″ in diameter, or No. 6 to No. 8 wood screw in a matching lead anchor.	Do not hang heavy weights on thick plaster unless you reach brick or other sturdy material behind it; if so, use a fastener appropriate to that material.
Brick	If brick is concealed behind plaster, white dust, possibly followed by the wood dust of thin furring strips, then brick dust. Heavy resistance as brick dust appears. A bit less than 3″ long does not break through.	Lead anchor with No. 6 to No. 8 wood screw long enough to reach 1″ into brick, or expansion shield with ¼″-diameter machine screw.	Lead anchor with No. 10 wood screw long enough to reach 1½″ into brick, or expansion shield with ¼″-diameter machine screw. For a very heavy load, lag anchor with lag screw ¼″ in diameter and 2″ to 3″ long.
Hollow tile	If tile blocks are concealed behind plaster, white dust followed by red dust. Heavy resistance as red dust appears, then drill bit breaks through.	Toggle bolt ¼″ in diameter. (Caution: Probe with wire to be sure there is space inside tile block for toggle wings to open.)	Toggle bolt ¼″ in diameter. (Caution: Probe with wire to be sure there is space inside tile block for toggle wings to open.)
Concrete or solid parts of cinderblock or concrete block	If blocks or concrete are concealed behind plaster, white dust, then gray or brownish gray dust. Heavy resistance as the darker dust appears. A bit less than 3″ long probably does not break through.	Lead anchor with No. 6 to No. 8 wood screw long enough to reach 1″ into concrete or block.	Expansion shield with machine screw ¼″ or greater in diameter. For a very heavy load, lag anchor with lag screw ¼″ in diameter and up to 6″ long.
Hollow sections of cinderblock or concrete block	Dust and resistance to drill as described immediately above, except the bit breaks through after penetrating the wall of the block.	Lead anchor fixed in the wall of the block with No. 6 to No. 8 wood screw; an expansion shield fixed in wall of block with ¼″-diameter machine screw; or toggle bolt ¼″ in diameter and long enough for wings to open inside block.	Toggle bolt ¼″ in diameter and long enough for wings to open inside block.

achieve a professional-looking standard of workmanship.

Whether you build or buy, racks and shelves are only as dependable as the means by which they are fastened in place. Kitchen tools are heavy: A set of cast-iron pots can weigh more than 100 pounds. Before you hang such a load on a wall or from the ceiling, you will want assurance that the shelf or rack holding the load is not going to suddenly come down. Luckily, the wooden framing members behind the wallboard walls and ceilings of most modern houses (page 37) provide firm anchorage. A storage unit that is given a secure grip on wall studs or ceiling joists by the correct screws or other fasteners is in place to stay.

You can find concealed studs and joists in various ways. Many carpenters swear they can locate a stud by rapping their knuckles across the wall: The wall sounds hollow except at studs, which — being dense — give a dull thud. Magnetic stud finders are widely available, but because they respond to metal — pipes and electric wiring as well as nails — they often give misleading readings. Electronic stud finders, which actually sense the density of any material behind the wallboard, are more accurate and are sold by several chains of department stores and do-it-yourself stores. An old-fashioned, but straightforward, technique for locating a stud or joist is shown on page 36. The technique requires drilling tiny holes in the wallboard, but you can easily fill these later with spackling compound.

Your walls, however, might be of some other type of construction, such as brick or cinderblock. In frame houses built before World War II, plaster was commonly troweled onto wood lath fixed to the studs. And in recently built apartment buildings, studs may be metal rather than wood. Suitable fasteners are available for almost all kinds of walls and ceilings. You can determine the type of construction you have — again, with a little drilling — by consulting the table opposite. The table will also tell you what fasteners are appropriate for that kind of construction. The following pages contain detailed drawings of the fasteners and instructions on how to use them.

To use fasteners such as Molly® bolts (page 41), you must know the exact thickness of the wallboard or other hollow-wall covering. To determine this, use a wire with its end bent into a hook. Insert the wire into a hole, and draw it back until the hook catches against the inside of the wall. Grasp the wire at the hole with thumb and forefinger to mark the wall thickness, then jiggle the hook free and pull the wire out. To use a toggle bolt (page 41), you must be sure there is enough space inside a hollow wall; to check it, probe through a hole with a straight wire.

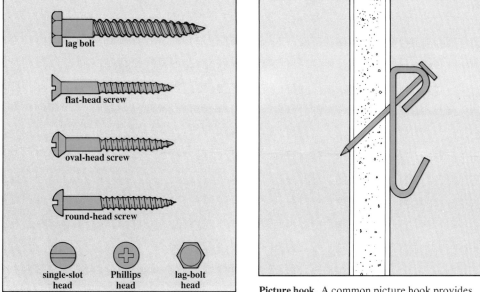

lag bolt

flat-head screw

oval-head screw

round-head screw

single-slot head | Phillips head | lag-bolt head

Wood screws. Flat-head wood screws are countersunk flush with the surrounding surface or hidden beneath plugs or putty. Round and oval heads can be left exposed. Heads have one slot or, for a Phillips screwdriver, two crossed indentations. Phillips heads are less likely to rip under turning pressure. Screw-shaft diameters are denoted by gauge numbers: The higher the number, the larger the diameter. The diameters of heavy-duty lag bolts, whose hexagonal (shown) or square heads are turned by wrenches, are expressed in inches (from ¼ to 1 inch).

Picture hook. A common picture hook provides an easy way to hang a light object on a wall. Large picture hooks, with nails long enough to reach through the wallboard into a stud, can support relatively heavy weights. (Load limits are printed on the packages.) Hold the hook against the wall, with the nail inserted at its downward angle through the holes, and hammer the nail home.

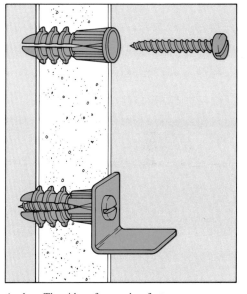

Anchor. The sides of an anchor fastener press out to gain a tight grip in masonry, wallboard or plaster when a matching-size screw is driven into it. A plastic anchor (above), sufficient for light loads, can be used with a wood screw or a self-tapping sheet-metal screw (shown). Heavier weights require lead anchors. With either type, first tap the anchor into a hole drilled to fit it snugly. (In wallboard, as here, the anchor and screw should be long enough to extend through it.) Then insert the screw through the object to be hung, and drive it into the anchor.

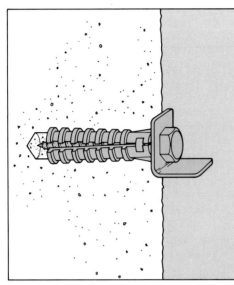

Lag bolt. Sometimes called a lag screw, this big fastener holds a very heavy load. To use it in a stud, drill a pilot hole slightly smaller in diameter than the bolt. Slip the bolt through the hanger of the object to be hung, then drive it into the hole by turning its head with a wrench. In masonry (*shown*), drill a hole deep enough for the bolt and wide enough so a matching-sized lag shield fits tightly; the flanges at the outer end of the shield should bite into the masonry. Tap the shield into the hole before driving the bolt into the shield.

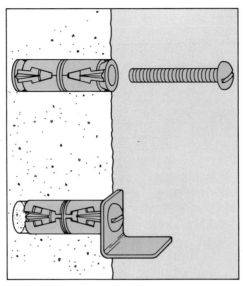

Expansion shield. This metal device with interior threads is used with a matching machine screw to hold a load on masonry or a thick plaster wall. Drill a hole that will hold the shield snugly, and tap the shield into it. Make sure the screw is long enough to extend through the hanger of the object being hung and the length of the shield. As you tighten the screw, wedges in the shield will be pulled toward the middle, pushing the cylinder sides hard against the masonry or plaster.

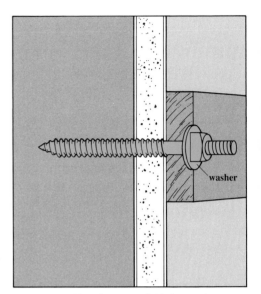

Hanger bolt. The advantage of this heavy-duty fastener is that you can fix it in the wall before the load is hung on it. One end is threaded like a wood screw, the other machine-threaded to take a nut. Drill a pilot hole slightly smaller than the bolt diameter into a stud. Drive the bolt in by turning it with locking-grip pliers grasping the middle section. Slip the hanging object over the protruding end and fasten it with a nut. If the hanging object is wood, as here, use a washer so the nut will not gouge the wood surface.

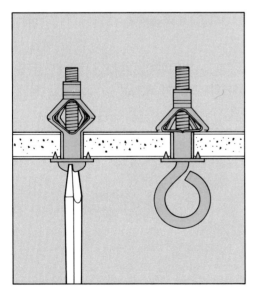

Ceiling Molly bolts and toggles. A Molly bolt (*above*) can hang light loads from a wallboard ceiling. Install a Molly bolt as you would in a wall (*opposite*). Then remove the bolt and replace it with an eye bolt of matching size. (An eye bolt, like a Molly bolt, has machine-screw threads; a screw eye that is threaded like a wood screw will not work.) Toggle bolts with swag hooks are available for ceilings. Screw the swag hook onto the unwinged end of the bolt before putting the bolt in the hole (*opposite*).

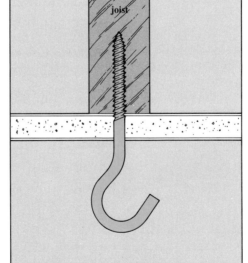

Ceiling hook. Heavy loads hung from a ceiling should be attached to strong screw hooks (or screw eyes) twisted directly into joists. For a load of up to 20 pounds, use a screw hook with a shaft $3/16$ inch in diameter and long enough to penetrate at least 1 inch into the joist. A $1/4$-inch-diameter screw hook that reaches 2 inches into the joist should hold a load of up to 50 pounds. For a $3/16$-inch hook, drill a $1/16$-inch pilot hole; for a $1/4$-inch hook, a $1/8$-inch hole. When twisting the screw in, use a wrench gripping the hook (or a screwdriver slipped through the screw eye) for leverage.

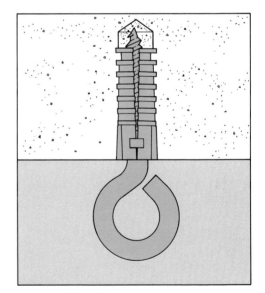

Ceiling lag shield. The same lag shields that are used in masonry walls (*see* **Lag bolt,** *above*) can hold large screw hooks or screw eyes of matching size in a concrete ceiling. As when dealing with a wall, tap the shield into a hole bored to fit it snugly and deep enough to take the screw shaft, and then screw in the hook or eye. A $1/4$-inch-diameter screw hook or eye in a shield that reaches at least $1/2$ inches into sound concrete should be able to hold up to 20 pounds.

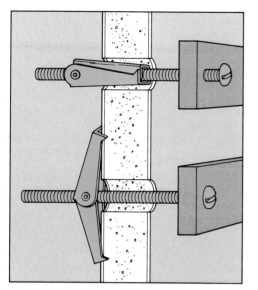

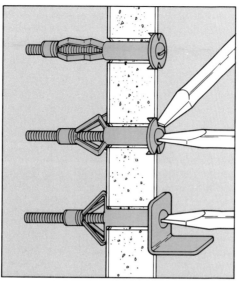

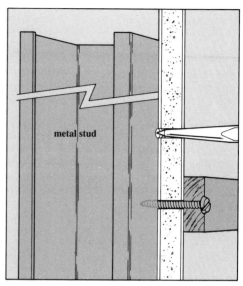

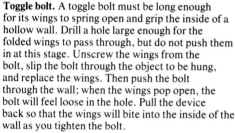

Toggle bolt. A toggle bolt must be long enough for its wings to spring open and grip the inside of a hollow wall. Drill a hole large enough for the folded wings to pass through, but do not push them in at this stage. Unscrew the wings from the bolt, slip the bolt through the object to be hung, and replace the wings. Then push the bolt through the wall; when the wings pop open, the bolt will feel loose in the hole. Pull the device back so that the wings will bite into the inside of the wall as you tighten the bolt.

Molly bolt. The unbroken cylinder near the bolthead of one of these hollow-wall anchors should be as long as the wall is thick. Tap the Molly bolt into a hole drilled to its diameter. Wedge a screwdriver into one of the indentations in the flange to keep the sheath from turning as you tighten the bolt with another screwdriver. The sheath arms will splay out against the inside of the wall. Do not overtighten, or you may break the Molly bolt's arms. Remove the bolt to put the load on it, then screw it back into position.

Self-tapping screw. This sort of screw is used to attach weights to metal studs. Drill a small hole in the wallboard to the face of the stud. Make a starter dent in the stud with a center punch and a hammer. Then use a high-speed-steel bit to drill a pilot hole half the diameter of the screw through the thin metal. Insert the screw through the object you are hanging, and drive it into the stud; the screw should be long enough to reach about ½ inch beyond the face of the stud.

Buying Lumber

As a rule, a good lumberyard is the best place to buy wood for whatever shelves, racks or other projects you undertake. Lumberyards carry a greater variety than other dealers do, and they are usually better equipped to cut wood to the sizes you want — although you should expect to pay extra for that service.

Most of the racks and shelves on the following pages call for softwood boards: lumber cut from pine or other needle-leaved trees. Ask for top-graded clear, or select, softwood and explain what you want it for, including whether you plan to paint the finished product or give it a natural finish. Specify kiln-dried lumber: It is less likely than air-dried wood to shrink or warp.

You will want boards that are dressed (planed smooth) on all four sides (S4S in lumber merchant's parlance). Softwood is normally sold that way. The nominal thickness and width of a board — the dimensions by which it is commonly de- scribed — are based on its predressed size. Thus, what is known as a 1-by-6 should be ¾ inch thick and 5½ inches wide by the time it is sold. However, the true dimensions of dressed lumber may vary. When boards are meant to fit to- gether, beware of buying one 1-by-6 that is actually, say, 5⅜ inches wide and an- other that is 5⅝ inches wide.

If you wish to substitute hardwood (cut from broad-leaved trees, such as oak) because of the beauty of its grain or color, ask for lumber graded firsts and seconds (FAS). Again, be certain it is kiln-dried. Sometimes hardwood is sold dressed only on two or three sides (S2S or S3S), so specify four sides smooth.

Some projects in this book call for plywood. For a natural finish, the best choice is hardwood plywood ("hard- wood" describes the surface plies; the inner layers may be softwood). Blem- ishes on the outer plies determine the grade. The finest hardwood surface is designated A, followed by B, then 2. Each surface is graded separately. If both will be visible, look for AA hard- wood plywood. But if only one side will show, you can save money by choosing A2 and hiding the grade 2 surface.

If the project is to be painted, you may want to use less expensive construction plywood — often called softwood ply- wood. The highest-quality surface is graded N, followed by A through D. AA usually takes paint well, although you may need to seal and prime it. Construc- tion plywood generally is sold in 8-by-4- foot sheets. More costly hardwood ply- woods can be bought in smaller pieces.

Before paying for any wood — or hav- ing the lumberyard saw it to size — in- spect it. Measure its thickness and width, sight along it to see if it is warped and examine all surfaces for defects. You should not purchase anything with- out seeing it first; if the dealer disagrees, try another lumberyard.

A wall rack from wood strips

The sleek wall rack shown here is a good way to augment storage space in a kitchen with a patch of unused wall. This particular version is almost 3 feet wide by 4 feet high, but the simplicity of the design — a ladder of narrow rails with equally narrow supports — will enable you to increase or decrease the overall dimensions to suit your purposes. The only stipulation for the adjustments is that the distance between vertical supports must never exceed 30 inches: Longer spans would be likely to break when weighted down.

The basic elements of the rack are ordinary pine 1-by-2s. To be stainable or paintable, the boards should be smooth, unblemished and as nearly knot-free as possible: The grades to order are clear or select. The boards will be sold by the running foot, usually in lengths of 8, 10 or 12 feet. But there will be some waste as the ends are squared, and each saw cut will remove 1/16 inch or so. The measurements for this rack (box, right) are designed to minimize trimming waste; the lumberyard can help you to make the most economical use of the board lengths.

The dealer also can saw the boards to your specifications; ask to have all of the ends cut square. Or you can size the boards yourself with a backsaw and a rock-maple miter box, as shown here, measuring each board as you go to guarantee precision.

Each rail of the rack must be positioned with geometric accuracy, making a carpenter's square invaluable at every step. Even so, minute differences of width and thickness among 1-by-2s dictate cutting the supports somewhat longer than you anticipate will be necessary and trimming them to fit at the end.

The joints in the rack are as simple as its design: lap joints, in which boards are attached where they lap over one another. For stability, these joints are best secured with glue and with flat-head screws driven into paired pilot holes: The holes in the rail are made with an adjustable counterbore bit for a No. 8 wood screw and are tapered at the top to recess the screwheads; the straight holes in the support are drilled with a 1/8-inch twist bit.

Before the rack is finished, the recesses above the screws are filled with wood putty — precolored if the rack is to be stained. When the finish is dry, the rack is ready to be mounted on the wall with whatever fastener is appropriate (pages 38-41). At this stage, a carpenter's level is essential, so you can make certain that the rack hangs straight.

Now all you need to do is add hooks. Ready-made hooks are, of course, available in a plethora of sizes and styles, but for custom effect you can use hooks of your own making, as shown below and in the box on page 45.

Materials List	
1 x 2	clear pine 1 x 2, 75', cut into:
	21 rails, 35" long
	3 supports, 48" long
Screws	63 No. 8 flat-head wood screws, 1½" long
Putty	wood putty
Finish	wood-finishing oil

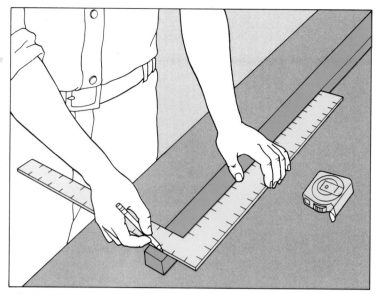

1 **Creating a square edge.** To square the end of a board, set a carpenter's square on top of it, positioning the square with the inside edge of its long leg lying against the side of the board and the outside edge of its short leg about an inch from the board's end. Using the square as a straightedge, draw a cutting line across the board.

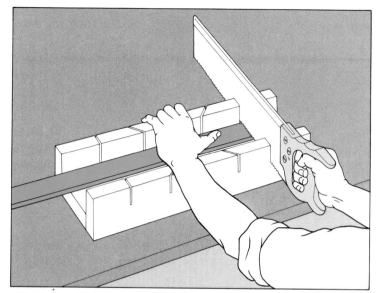

2 **Cutting the pieces.** Set the board flat in a miter box, and slide a backsaw into the box's right-angled slots. Place the waste side of the board's pencil line against the saw blade, hold the board tightly against the back of the miter box, and saw along the line. Measure, mark and cut all of the 35-inch rails similarly, then all of the 48-inch supports. Using medium (100-grit) sandpaper, smooth the edges and ends of the boards.

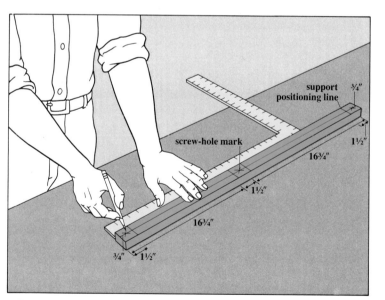
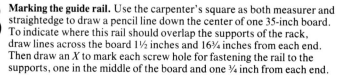

3 **Marking the guide rail.** Use the carpenter's square as both measurer and straightedge to draw a pencil line down the center of one 35-inch board. To indicate where this rail should overlap the supports of the rack, draw lines across the board 1½ inches and 16¾ inches from each end. Then draw an X to mark each screw hole for fastening the rail to the supports, one in the middle of the board and one ¾ inch from each end.

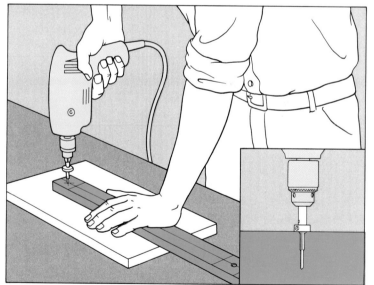

4 **Drilling countersunk screw holes.** Insert an adjustable counterbore bit for a 1½-inch No. 8 wood screw into a power drill (*inset, above, and page 125, top*). Set the guide rail on a piece of scrap wood, with one of the marked screw holes above the scrap. Holding the board steady, drill all the way through the wood at the mark. Then repeat the process to drill the other marked holes.

Using the drilled guide rail as a pattern, set it on each of the other 35-inch boards in turn. Mark the position of the holes onto the bottom board with a pencil. When the screw holes in all of the 35-inch rails are marked, drill countersunk holes in each board. ▶

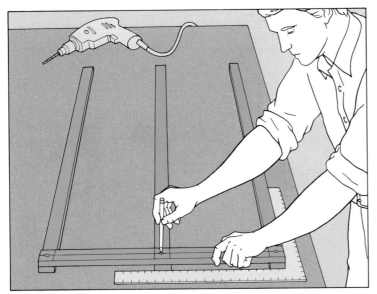

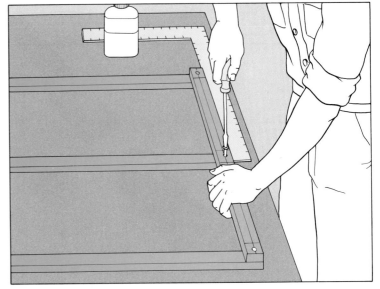

5 **Preparing the base of the supports.** Lay the three 4-foot boards that will form the supports of the rack on the work surface, parallel to one another. Place the guide rail, penciled side up, at one end of — and perpendicular to — the three supports. Adjust the positions of the supports until they match up with the vertical lines drawn on the guide; the angles at the left and right corners should be 90°. Insert a pencil through the countersunk holes of the guide to the supports below to mark the location of the pilot holes. Fit a ⅛-inch twist bit into the drill, and set the marked end of each support in turn on top of a piece of scrap wood; then drill through the support at the mark.

6 **Attaching the guide rail.** Put the three supports back on the work surface in approximately their correct positions, with the drilled ends toward you. Turn the guide rail penciled side down, and dab a ring of glue around each of its three screw holes. Turn the guide over, set it on top of the supports, and align them so that the screw holes meet and the corners are square. Drive a 1½-inch No. 8 flat-head screw into each hole. Lightly sand away the pencil marks, using fine (150-grit) sandpaper.

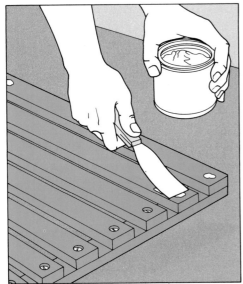

9 **Filling the screw holes.** Scoop a little bit of wood putty onto the tip of a putty knife. Press putty into each screw hole, overfilling it slightly to allow for shrinkage. Let the putty dry overnight, or until it feels dry and firm when pressed. Then use medium (100-grit) sandpaper to smooth the surface of the putty flush with the wood. Finish the rack with wood stain or paint.

10 **Leveling the rack.** Using a ¼-inch twist bit, drill four holes into the supports at the outside corners. Have a helper hold the rack against the wall in the position desired. Place a carpenter's level on top and adjust the position of the rack until the middle bubble in the level is centered. With a pencil, make a mark through each screw hole and onto the wall. Remove the rack, and drill holes at the points marked for the fasteners you will be using (pages 38-41). Then reposition the unit and attach it to the wall.

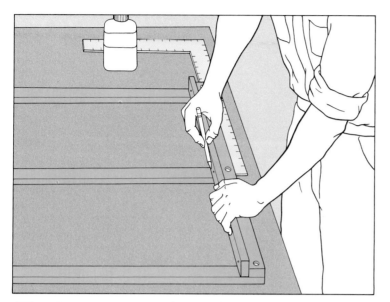

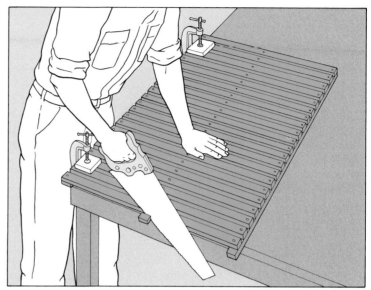

7 **Adding each subsequent rail.** Set a predrilled rail upright against the previously installed rail. To determine the space to leave between them, draw lines along the far edge of the second rail where it crosses the supports. Then lay the rail flat, with the beveled section of its holes upward and its near edge against the spacing lines. Make certain that the ends of the 1-by-2 are flush with the outside edges of the supports. Insert a pencil through each countersunk hole to mark the location for drilling; drill holes with a ⅛-inch twist bit, then glue and screw down the rail as described in Step 6.

8 **Trimming the supports.** When you have attached all 21 horizontal rails, clamp one side of the rack securely to the work surface, putting pieces of scrap wood between the rack and the clamps to protect the boards. Then use a handsaw to cut the tip off each support so that its end is flush with the top edge of the top rail. Sand the cut edges smooth.

Shaping a Brass Hook

With a little imagination, you can find an almost endless list of suppliers for the hooks you need on wall and ceiling racks. Hardware, housewares and kitchen-supply stores are the logical first stops on a shopping trip. Restaurant and retail-store suppliers have heavy-duty hooks; garden shops carry plant hooks that often can be adapted to use with pots and pans.

If you cannot find exactly the hooks you need, it is simple enough to buy brass rods ⅛ inch thick and bend them to fit your rack. Available in 12-inch lengths at hobby shops and some hardware stores, the rods are easily shaped with pliers, cut with wire cutters and polished smooth with a metal file.

In the demonstration at right, the top crook is ¾ inch wide to match the thickness of the 1-by-2 board it will rest on; the back is about 1 inch deep. The shank from the top to the bottom may be any desired length, and the bottom crook can be varied to make it commodious enough to secure whatever kitchen item it will hold.

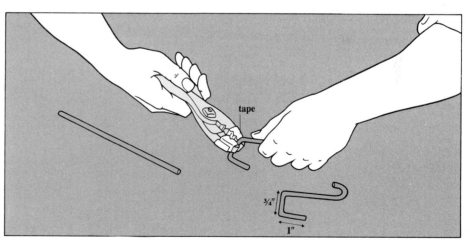
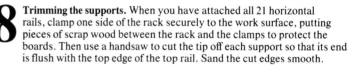

Bending the brass rod. Cut a 12-inch rod in half with wire cutters; file the cut edges smooth with a metalworking file. Wrap tape around the teeth of the pliers to protect the rod as it is being bent. Set the front teeth of the pliers over the rod about an inch from one end. Bend the rod until it forms a 90° angle. Then position the pliers about ½ inch in from the angle and bend the rod again, making sure that the space between the two angles is at least ¾ inch. Finally, grip the other end of the rod about ½ inch from the end and bend the rod upward to form the U-shaped crook from which the pots will hang.

A made-to-measure shelf gallery

Glass jars brimming with dried foodstuffs bring a singularly appropriate splash of color to a kitchen. Here they are displayed on a shelf unit created from pine boards cut to fit the particular containers it holds. To design similar shelves to fit objects you wish to put on view, first spread a large piece of heavy paper on a table. Lay the objects on the paper on their sides, as if they were standing on shelves, and shift them about until you achieve an arrangement you like.

Lightly pencil a rectangular outline around the object, or group of objects, that you plan to display in each shelf compartment. Allow sufficient space for moving objects onto the shelves easily.

Put the objects aside, and use a steel square to convert your rough sketch to an accurate plan that presents an edge-on view of the vertical and horizontal components of your shelf unit; your diagram should resemble the white edges on the drawing at right. Your boards will be nominally 1 inch thick, but draw them to their actual ¾-inch finished thickness.

To make assembling the shelves as easy as possible, the boards are screwed together in right-angle butt joints (that is, with the end of one board butting against the side of another, to which it is perpendicular). When drawing your plan, avoid positioning the ends of two boards directly opposite each other where they butt against the sides of a third; the joints must be staggered to be secured with screws.

When the diagram is complete, give each component an alphabetical designation. On the plan shown, the horizontal boards were labeled from top to bottom and the vertical boards from left to right. Next, write the whole length of each component on the plan. Then measure and note on the plan the distances between intersecting pieces along both sides of each component. On the underside of board C in this plan, for instance, there are 5 inches between boards G and H, 5 inches between H and I, and another 5 between I and J.

Measure the display objects or groups to determine how deep — front to back — your shelves must be. So-called 1-inch boards are available in widths ranging from 1½ to 11¼ inches (1-by-2 to 1-by-12). Then total the lengths of the components to determine how many running feet of lumber you need.

For butt joints, the ends of the boards must be precisely square-cut. To ensure this, have the lumberyard cut the boards to length; or, if you do the sawing, use a steel square as a straightedge (*page 43, Step 1*) to mark the cutting line across each board in turn. Then fix a straight wood strip to the board to guide a circular saw (*page 124*), set the blade at a 90° angle to the board, and saw along the line.

Do not try to cut the boards with a hand-held saw unless you have a miter box wide enough to hold the lumber; achieving squared cuts is extremely difficult when sawing freehand.

As soon as it is cut, mark each board with its letter designation from the diagram. Then label the two wide surfaces of each board, designating the top and bottom surfaces of horizontal components, the left and right sides of vertical pieces. Also mark each end of the board with the letter designation of the board that end will butt against. (Here, for example, the left end of board **C** should be marked **G**, and the right end **J**.) These markings — and others you add in Steps 1 and 2 of the following instructions — will be essential when you drill holes for the screws that will join the boards.

To hang the finished unit on a wall, fix it at all four corners with appropriate fasteners *(pages 38-41)*. At least one vertical pair of fasteners — both pairs if the shelves are to carry a heavy load — should be attached to a wall stud. If none of the corners lines up with a stud, add an extra pair of hangers that will. If there is no backsplash to get in the way, you might want to design your shelves to fit beneath wall cabinets at the back of a counter. Since the counter will bear the weight, you will need to fix the unit to the wall only at the two upper corners, using fasteners appropriate for a light load.

The list of materials below and the step-by-step instructions that follow are for the shelves shown here, but they can easily be adapted to the shelves you design.

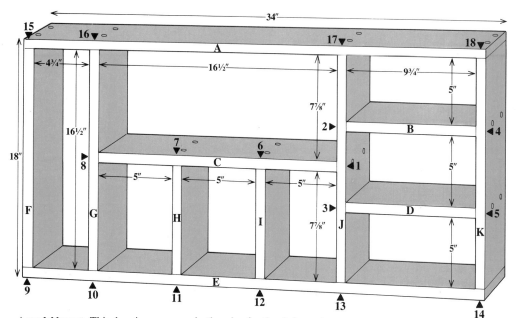

A model layout. This drawing serves as both a plan for the shelves at left and a guide for developing your own arrangement. These shelves are made of 1-by-6 pine boards, cut to the lengths shown. The letters identify the boards, and the boldface numbers give a sequence for assembling them so you never have to maneuver in an awkwardly tight space to drive the screws that hold boards together. Letter and number your own plan similarly. The black triangle at each joint indicates the direction of the counterbored screw holes for that joint. When the unit is completed, hanger plates are screwed to the back of the shelves.

Materials List

1 x 6	16' clear pine 1 x 6, cut into: 2 boards (**A** and **E**), 34" long 5 boards (**C, F, G, J** and **K**), 16½" long 2 boards (**H** and **I**), 7⅞" long 2 boards (**B** and **D**), 9¾" long
Screws	36 No. 10 flat-head wood screws, 1¾" long 8 No. 6 flat-head wood screws, 1" long
Hangers	4 hanger plates, 2" long
Putty	wood putty; for oil-finished shelves, a putty that will accept a stain
Finish	paint or oil stain

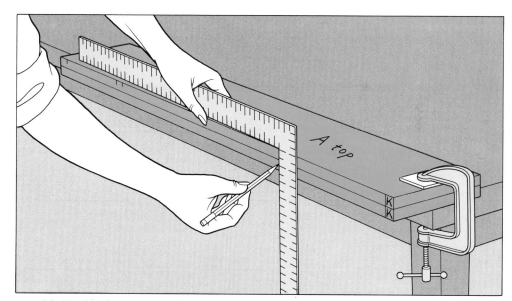

1 **Marking butt-joint positions.** Cut and label all of the boards for the shelves. Stack the boards designated **A** and **E** — the pieces that will be the top and bottom horizontal pieces of the unit — with the bottom of board **A** and the top of board **E** facing each other. Using scrap wood to protect the boards, clamp them to the edge of the work surface. Measure along the edges of the boards to mark the ¾-inch-wide places where vertical boards will butt both of them. (Follow your own diagram; here boards **F, G, J** and **K** will butt both **A** and **E**.) Align one arm of the steel square with the top of board **A**, and use the other arm as a straightedge to draw vertical lines across the edges of the boards. Label each joint position with the letter for the intersecting board. ▶

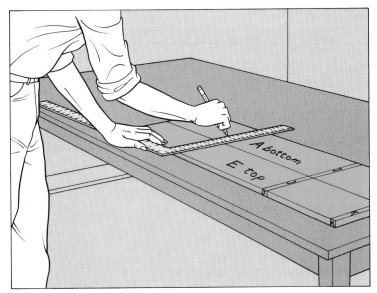

2 **Extending the joint lines.** Unclamp the boards, and flip board **A** back so it is bottom side up and lying snug alongside **E**. Align the ends of the boards. Then extend the pencil lines from the edge of **E** across both boards *(above),* using the steel square to make the lines perpendicular to the boards' edges. Identify each joint position by letter as you complete it. Now turn both boards end over end, so you can still see the lines on the near edge of board **E**, and extend the lines across the newly turned-up surfaces. Put an **X** within each pair of these last lines; the lines later will serve as guides for counterboring screw holes.

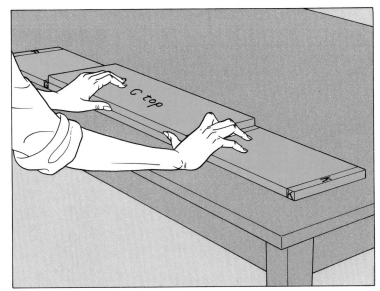

3 **Marking the other components.** Referring to your plan, pair up all the boards that will be butted by opposite ends of common perpendicular boards, and mark them as you marked the first two. Some boards will have to be paired and marked first with one mate and then with another. Board **E**, for instance, must also be marked in tandem with board **C** *(above),* because both are butted by the ends of vertical boards **H** and **I** *(diagram, page 47);* always clamp the boards together to match their relative position on the plan. When all of the boards have been marked, spread out your diagram and assemble them on it — standing them on their back edges in their designated positions — to make certain that their lengths and joint markings are correct.

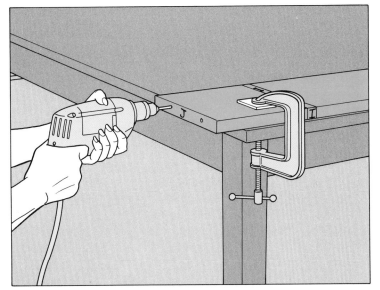

6 **Drilling the pilot holes.** Clamp a board to the worktable so that one marked end is facing you. Using a ⅛-inch twist bit, drill pilot holes about 1 inch deep at the marked places. Unclamp the board, and turn it around to drill pilot holes in the other end. Following the same procedure with other boards, drill all of the other pilot holes.

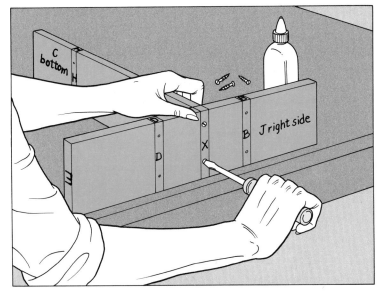

7 **Assembling the unit.** Find the two boards that will form the first joint in the assembly sequence numbered on your diagram. On the plan followed here, the first joint is formed where one end of board **C** butts against the left side of board **J**. In this case, squeeze one line of wood glue onto the end of board **C** that bears the initial **J** and another line onto the corresponding joint position on board **J**. Then butt the boards together, insert 1¾-inch No. 10 screws through the counterbored holes in **J**, and drive them into the end of board **C**. Turn the screws into the counterbores until the two boards are fixed tightly together. Following the sequence of numbered joints, fasten the rest of the boards in place with screws until the entire unit is assembled.

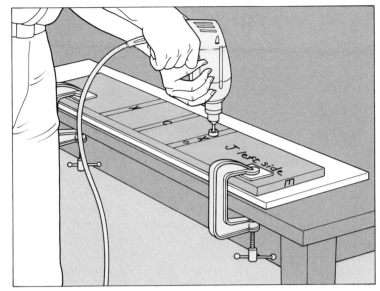

4 **Counterboring the screw holes.** Fit a power drill with an adjustable counterbore bit for a No. 10 screw, set to provide a ¼-inch-deep counterbore. Clamp a board that will be butted by the end of another board atop a piece of scrap lumber. Double-checking with your plan to make certain you are counterboring into the correct surface, drill two holes *(above)* within each pair of screw-hole guidelines, which were marked with an **X** in Step 2; place the holes midway between the lines and 1½ inches from the board's edges. Turn the board over, and drill any hole positions marked on the other side. Then go on to drill counterbored holes in all the other boards that require them.

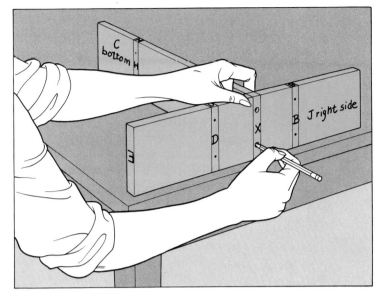

5 **Marking for pilot holes.** Place two boards that will form a butt joint on edge in their correct relative positions. (Refer to your diagram to be sure their ends and sides all face the right directions.) Hold the end of one board hard against its letter-identified joint position on the second. Slide the tip of a pencil through the counterbored holes in the second board *(above)* to mark the placement of pilot holes on the end of the first. Proceed to mark all the other butting ends the same way.

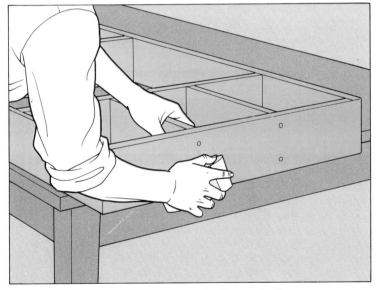

8 **Concealing the screwheads.** With the tip of a putty knife, scoop up a small amount of wood putty, and press it into each counterbored hole; if you will be staining the rack when it is completed, be sure to use a wood putty that will accept a stain. Overfill the holes slightly, because the putty will shrink as it dries. When the putty has dried — overnight, or when it feels dry and firm when pressed — sand it flush with the surface of the wood *(above)*, using medium (100-grit) sandpaper wrapped around a sanding block. Also sand any exposed ends of boards. Now paint the unit; if, instead, you are going to stain it, first erase the pencil marks or sand them away with fine (150-grit) sandpaper.

9 **Attaching the hanger plates.** Hold a hanger plate against a corner joint at the back of the shelves so the hanger's loop extends beyond the top of the unit while one of its holes is positioned on a horizontal component and the other on a vertical board. Mark the hole positions on the back of the unit as shown. Mark hole positions on the other top corner, the two bottom corners, and any other places where hangers will be attached. Using a ³⁄₃₂-inch twist bit, drill pilot holes about 1 inch deep at each marked place. Then drive 1-inch No. 6 wood screws through the holes in the plates into the pilot holes. The shelves are now ready to be hung on the wall with appropriate fasteners.

Adjustable shelves for a window garden

Y ou can turn any kitchen window into a multitiered indoor garden with a plant rack like this one. The supports are mounted outside the window's frame, so the rack fits at a shallow window as well as it does at a deeply recessed one. To set the shelves at different heights, you can simply pull out the wood dowels that hold them, move the shelf strips to new positions, then reinsert the dowels. And — because of its airy, layered construction — the rack lets in the sunshine.

Make the rack from 1-by-2 pine strips, available at lumberyards in standard 8-, 10- or 12-foot lengths. You can have the strips cut to size by the dealer, or cut them at home using a miter box and a hand-held backsaw (page 43).

The strip lengths used in the rack shown here — for a window 38 by 54 inches — are detailed in the materials list at top right, but you should modify the dimensions to fit your own window. The back-support strips (right) should be as long as the window is high, from the sill to the top of the frame. Subtract 6 inches from the window height to find the length of the side-panel strips. To determine the length of the shelf strips, measure the width of the window frame (from outside edge to outside edge), then add 4 inches.

When you bore the holes for the height-adjustment dowels, use a power drill fitted with a ⅜-inch spade bit and a drill guide, which keeps the bit straight as it moves through the wood. (These special tools are described on page 125.) You will also need adjustable countersink bits to fit both a No. 10 and a No. 8 wood screw, a ⅛-inch twist bit, a steel tape measure or steel ruler, wood glue and wood screws, C clamps, a carpenter's level, and fine (150-grit) sandpaper.

Before hanging the rack, locate the studs that frame the window opening (pages 36-37). You probably will be able to attach the rack to these studs with 2-inch round-head screws. (Remember, most windows are flanked by double studs; be certain you drive the screws into studs, and not into the crack between studs.) If you cannot find studs where you need them, use appropriate alternative wall fasteners (pages 38-41).

Materials List

1 x 2	100′ clear pine 1 x 2, cut into:
	2 back-support strips, 54″ long
	8 side-panel strips, 48″ long
	15 shelf strips, 42″ long
	12 spacing blocks, 3″ long

Dowels	2 ⁵⁄₁₆″ dowels, 36″ long, cut into 10 6″ lengths

Screws	16 No. 10 flat-head wood screws, 2″ long
	8 No. 8 flat-head wood screws, 1¼″ long

Finish	wood-finishing oil

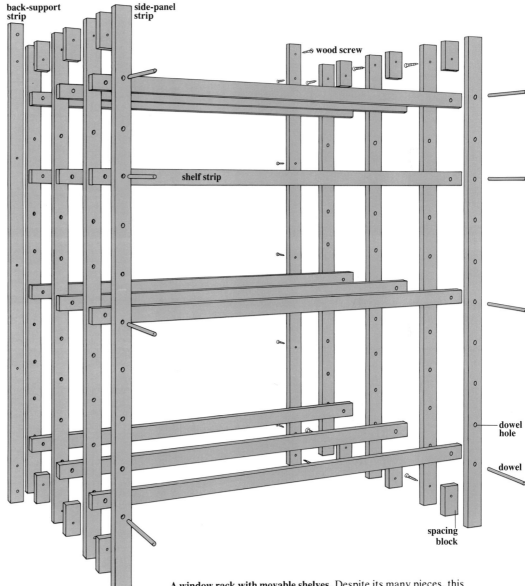

back-support strip

side-panel strip

wood screw

shelf strip

dowel hole

dowel

spacing block

A window rack with movable shelves. Despite its many pieces, this rack is very simply built. Each side panel is made of four vertical strips separated by spacing blocks, but bound with wood glue and screws. The side panels are attached to support strips, which are fastened to the wall. The shelf strips slip through the spaces in the side panels, then are held in place by dowels pushed through holes in the side panels. ▶

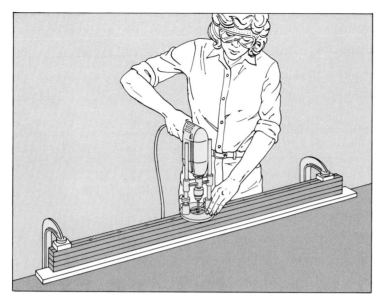

1 **Drilling dowel holes in side strips.** Lightly pencil a line along the center of one side strip. Then mark positions along this line for dowel holes 6 inches from each end and at 4-inch intervals in between. Stack the marked strip atop three others and a piece of scrap wood. Align the edges of the strips, and anchor the stack to the work surface with C clamps, using wood scraps to protect the top strip from the clamps. Fit a power drill with a drill guide *(page 125)* and a ⅜-inch spade bit. Wearing safety goggles, bore straight through all four strips at each dowel-hole mark. Sand off all pencil marks. Now make a stack of the other four side strips, and mark the dowel-hole positions on the top strip by using one of the drilled pieces as a guide. Clamp and drill that stack.

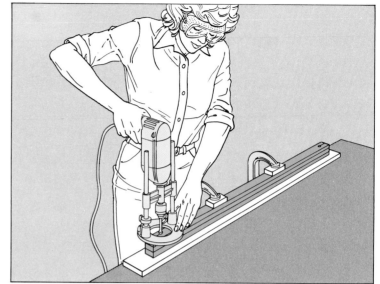

2 **Drilling dowel holes in the shelf strips.** Draw lines across a shelf strip 1½ inches from each end and make a mark for a dowel hole at the exact center of each line. Put the marked strip atop two other shelf strips and a piece of scrap wood. Align the edges of the strips and secure them to the work surface with C clamps, protecting the strips with scrap wood; drill the dowel holes as in Step 1. Then sand off the pencil marks. Next, use one of the drilled pieces to transfer the dowel-hole positions onto the top strip of another stack of three; clamp that stack, and drill the holes. Drill the remaining two sets of three strips in the same way, keeping the sets separate from one another to ensure that all of the holes in each shelf will be perfectly aligned.

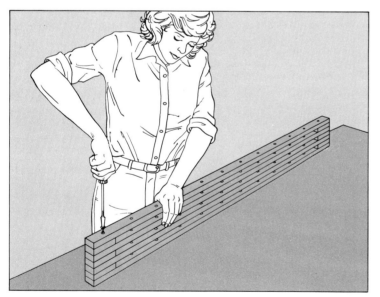

4 **Completing a side panel.** Place a second layer of spacing blocks and a third side strip on top of those assembled in Step 3. Clamp the unit to the work surface, and drill countersunk holes through the top strip and the spacing blocks and into the middle strip, locating the holes so the drill bit does not hit the screws already inserted in the middle strip. Attach the new pieces with glue and screws, then add the final layer *(above)*, again making sure you do not drill into the screws below.

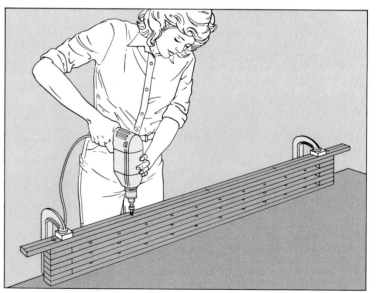

5 **Attaching the support strip.** Center a back-support strip on top of the side panel, with the sides aligned and the ends of the strip extending 3 inches beyond the ends of the panel. Adjust the countersink bit to fit a No. 8 screw. Drill a 1¼-inch hole through the strip into each end of the panel, avoiding the screws below; drill additional holes at 12-inch intervals all along the support strip to hold additional screws for a secure bond. Then, with a ¼-inch twist bit, drill holes at the center line 2 inches from the overhanging ends of the strip; the rack will be held to the wall through these holes. Unclamp the strip, apply wood glue to its underside and reposition it on the side panel. Fasten it with No. 8 screws. Assemble the other side panel and support strip in the same way.

3 **Spacing the side strips.** On a piece of scrap wood, sandwich two spacing blocks between the ends of two side strips. Slip a small piece of scrap wood, the same thickness as the blocks, into the middle; then use a C clamp to hold all the pieces to the worktable as shown; be sure the sides and ends of the strips and spacing blocks are flush. With an adjustable countersink bit set to fit a No. 10 screw *(page 43)*, drill a 2-inch hole at each end — from the top strip all the way through the bottom strip. Unclamp the strips, apply wood glue to both surfaces of each spacing block, reposition the pieces and drive the screws through the holes.

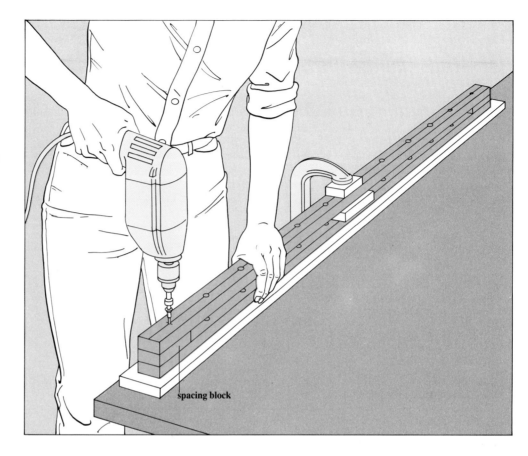

spacing block

6 **Assembling the shelves.** Round off the ends of the dowels with sandpaper so they will slip easily through the dowel holes. Set the two side panels parallel to each other on their back-support strips. Position the first set of shelf strips, making sure that the holes on the shelf strips are aligned with the holes in the panel, and insert dowels through the lined-up holes *(right)*. Decide where you want the remaining shelves and attach them to the side panels with dowels. Finally, hang the rack on the wall.

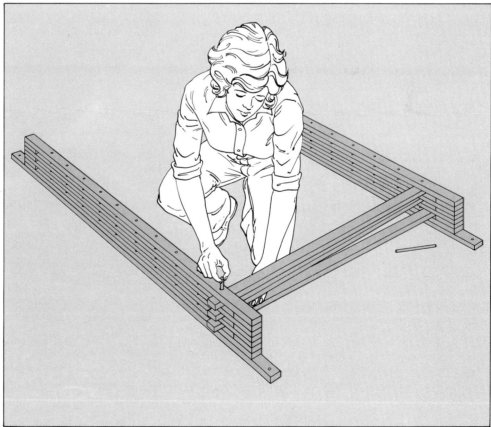

The grace of curves from plywood and dowels

The sandwich construction of plywood makes it possible for you to cut design elements that narrow as much as the sides of this rack do — without having the wood split or crack under your saw. Here, the sides of the rack swoop upward and outward in a graceful arc, along which are suspended wood dowel supports for kitchen tools.

At the top of the rack, a shelf offers extra space for storage or display.

For naturally colored surfaces with handsome graining and a smoothness that simplifies finishing, use hardwood plywood for the sides, top and back braces of the rack. Adhesive-backed veneer banding, available in most hardwoods, will cover up the edges of the plies.

Maple, oak, cherry or the birch plywood shown here are all suitable; but be certain your choice is labeled AA, indicating that both surfaces are of top (A) quality. Softwood plywoods, such as fir or pine, are a money saver if you prefer a painted rack, but you will still want to buy AA quality for its smoothness.

Ask your wood supplier to cut the ply-

wood into rectangles of the sizes specified in the materials list *(right)*. Or cut them yourself with a circular saw. (The use of this and other special tools is described on pages 122-125.) In either case, make sure that the grain of the veneer runs lengthwise in each piece.

To produce the curved side pieces, you will need to draw a template *(overleaf)* on a large piece of cardboard with the aid of a carpenter's square and a compass. Transfer the pattern to the wood, and cut it with a saber saw.

This rack incorporates standard 36-inch-long dowels. Some manufacturers tip one end of each dowel with a color designating its diameter. If you plan to stain the dowels, as shown here, saw an inch off that end of every dowel.

You can modify the vertical dimensions of the rack or narrow it to suit your needs. Simply make sure that the back braces are 2½ inches shorter than your dowel lengths, and that the top shelf is 1 inch longer than your dowels. However, do not make your rack wider than this one: Longer dowels might bend from the weight of items hung on them.

The holes for the dowels are cut with a drill mounted on a special drill guide that ensures the bit moves straight through the wood. For the drill, you will need a ⅛-inch twist bit, a ⅝-inch spade bit and an adjustable counterbore for a No. 8 wood screw to cut recessed screw holes. In addition to saws, hammer and screwdriver, other necessary tools are C clamps, a wood shaver, a sanding block and an electric iron.

These instructions show you how to fasten the rack to a brick wall. To determine the appropriate fasteners for other kinds of walls, see pages 38-41. If you are hanging the rack on a wall that has studs, make sure that at least one hanger is secured to a stud. You may have to add a third hanger to accommodate the location of the stud.

Materials List

Plywood	1 piece AA-quality ¾'' birch plywood, 4' x 4', cut into:		**Banding**	¾'' birch-veneer iron-on banding, 24'
	2 side pieces, 10½'' x 33''		**Screws**	17 No. 8 flat-head wood screws, 1½'' long
	1 top back brace, 3½'' x 32½''			
	1 bottom back brace, 2½'' x 32½''		**Stain**	oil-based wood stain
	1 shelf, 11½'' x 36''			
Dowels	18 ⅝'' wood dowels, 3' long		**Hangers**	2 heavy-duty mirror hangers, 3'' long, ⅝'' wide
Plugs	16 ⅜'' wood plugs, ⅜'' long			

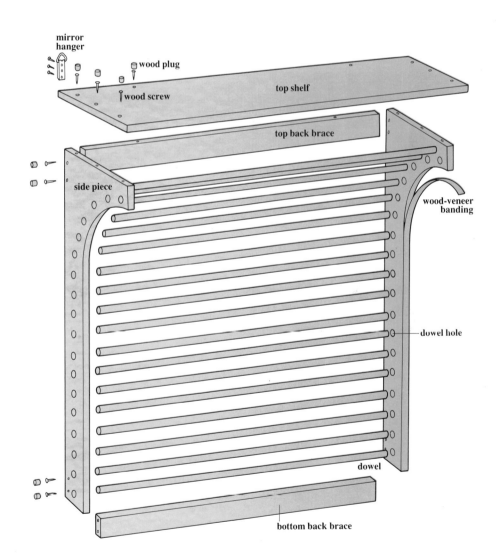

A wood dowel rack. The horizontal rods of this rack are wood dowels suspended in a plywood frame. The side pieces are braced in the back at top and bottom, and on the top by a shelf that overhangs each side by 1 inch. The frame is held together with wood screws hidden by wood plugs. Iron-on veneer banding covers all exposed edges of the plywood. Heavy-duty hangers are screwed into the back of the rack. ▶

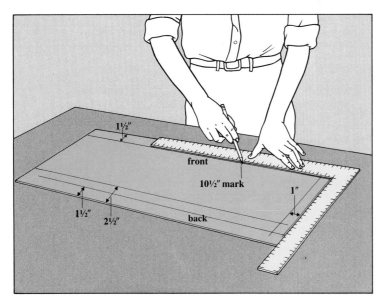

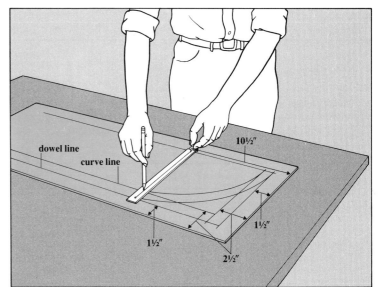

1 **Beginning the template.** Using a soft-lead pencil and a carpenter's square to make perfect right angles, draw a rectangle 12 inches wide and 33 inches long on heavy cardboard. Cut out the rectangle with a utility knife, laying the carpenter's square along the lines to serve as a straight-edge. Then draw straight lines the length of the cardboard, parallel to and 1½ inches from the back and front edges. At the back, draw another parallel line 2½ inches from the edge. Now draw two parallel lines across the top of the rectangle — 1½ inches and 2½ inches from the end.

2 **Drawing the curved lines.** Make a pencil mark on the front line 10½ inches from the top edge. Cut a strip of cardboard 2 inches wide and 11 inches long. Draw a line down the center of the strip, and then punch holes along this line 1½ and 2½ inches in from one end and ½ inch in from the opposite end. Use a pushpin to attach the strip to the 10½-inch mark through the hole at the ½-inch mark. Then insert the tip of a pencil into the hole at the 1½-inch mark. Holding the pencil upright, swing the strip in an arc to draw the curve of a line to locate the dowel positions. Then place the pencil tip in the hole at the 2½-inch mark and draw another arc for cutting the curve of the side piece.

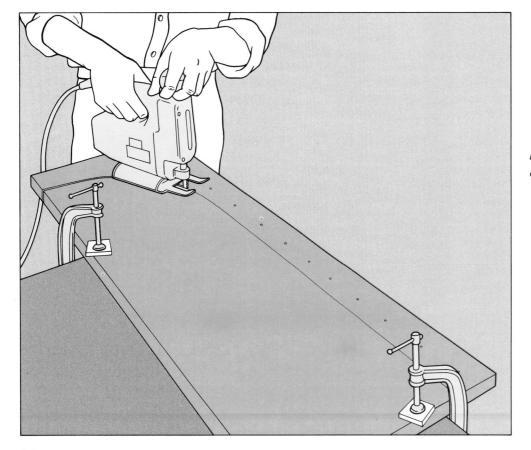

5 **Cutting the side pieces.** Position one side piece on a work surface, with the curved line beyond the edge of the surface. Anchor the side piece with C clamps, setting small scraps of wood between the plywood and the clamp's jaws to protect the birch. Wearing safety goggles, cut along the curved line with a saber saw (left), moving the saw slowly to ensure a smooth arc; as the cut progresses, have a helper support the freed end of the side piece to prevent it from splitting away. Remove the pieces, clamp the second side piece into place and saw its curved line.

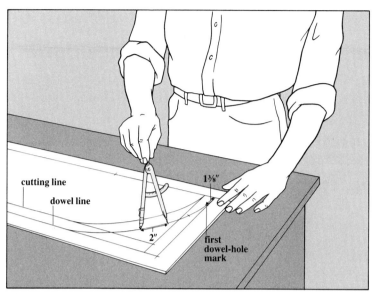

3 **Marking the dowel-hole positions.** Set the tips of a compass 1⅜ inches apart. Place the sharp compass leg at the front edge of the dowel line, and use the pencil-tipped leg to draw a small arc across the dowel line; the intersection of arc and line marks the position of the first dowel hole. Reset the compass so that its tips are 2 inches apart. With the sharp leg on the first dowel mark, draw another arc across the dowel line and then move the sharp leg to that spot. Continue drawing arcs and moving the compass along the line at 2-inch intervals. Then punch a hole at each dowel position with a nail. Now use a utility knife to cut out the template along the cutting line shown above.

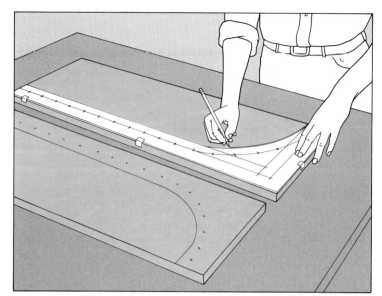

4 **Transferring the pattern.** Lay the two plywood side pieces next to each other, and position the template on one of them. Align the top and back edges of the template and wood, then tape the template in place. Trace the template's curved edge onto the wood with a pencil. Then push the pencil tip into each hole in the template to mark the dowel positions. Flip the template over onto the second piece of wood so that the curved edge faces the direction opposite that of the first piece. Now transfer the curved line and hole marks onto this piece.

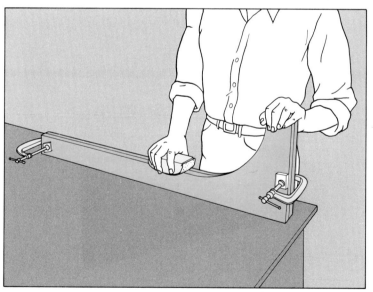

6 **Sanding the edges.** Align the side pieces and clamp them together, again using scrap wood to protect the birch. Using fine (150-grit) sandpaper, smooth the curved edges, the straight upper front edges and the bottom edges; keep the sanding block flat, and move it back and forth slowly. Do not round off edges or corners, or the veneer banding will not adhere properly.

Replacing the sandpaper as needed, sand the edges of the other pieces of the rack that will be veneered: the front and both ends of the top shelf, the long edges of the bottom back brace, and the lower long edge of the top back brace. Wipe off all sanding dust.

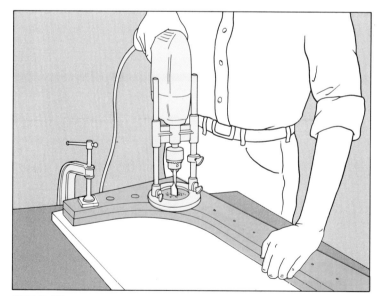

7 **Drilling the dowel holes.** Put the side pieces atop a big piece of scrap wood, and clamp them securely to the work surface. The scrap wood will keep the plywood from splintering as the drill bit breaks through. Fit a power drill with a drill guide and a ⅝-inch spade bit (page 125). Wearing safety goggles, center the bit over one of the dowel-hole marks; drill straight through both pieces. Repeat at each mark. ▶

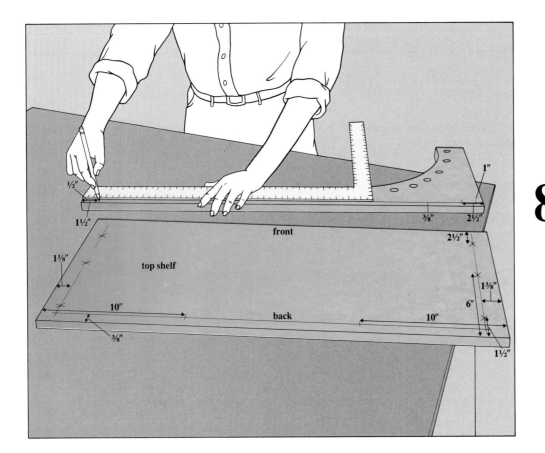

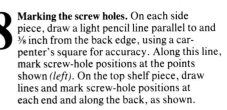

8 Marking the screw holes. On each side piece, draw a light pencil line parallel to and ⅜ inch from the back edge, using a carpenter's square for accuracy. Along this line, mark screw-hole positions at the points shown *(left)*. On the top shelf piece, draw lines and mark screw-hole positions at each end and along the back, as shown.

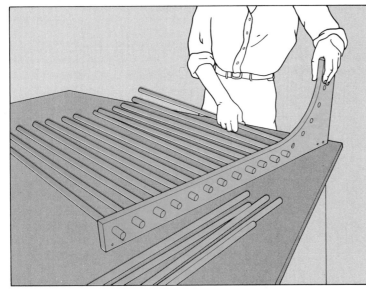

12 Inserting the dowels into a side piece. Pile the dowels within arm's reach. Place one of the side pieces on its back edge on the work surface. Insert the dowels into the holes along one face of the side piece. Twist and push the dowels through until they extend about ½ to 1 inch beyond the other face of the side piece.

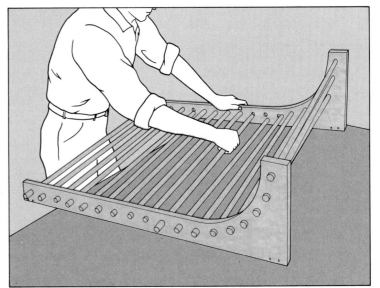

13 Putting on the second side piece. Line up the second side piece with the free ends of the dowels. Starting at the top end of the rack, twist the first few dowels into their holes, inserting them as far as you can without pulling them out of the holes of the other side piece. Some of the dowels may fit too snugly for you to push them all the way through the holes; just make sure their tips are securely anchored. Then start pushing dowels into holes at the bottom end of the second side and continue working up the rack until all the dowels are at least partly inserted.

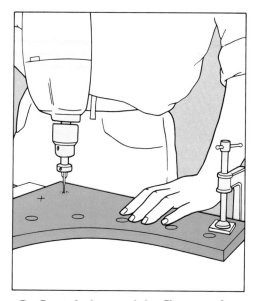

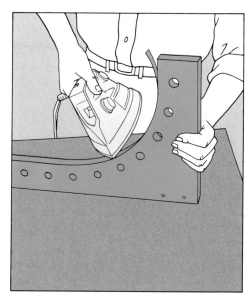

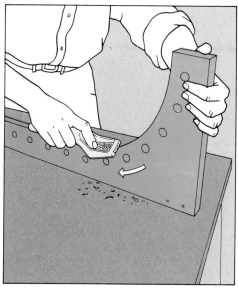

9 Counterboring screw holes. Clamp one of the side pieces atop a piece of scrap wood on the work surface. Fit your electric drill with an adjustable counterbore drill bit for a 1½-inch No. 8 wood screw. Then, wearing safety goggles, drill straight into the screw-hole marks until the collar stops the downward motion. After drilling all of the screw holes for the two sides, drill the ones marked on the top shelf piece.

10 Ironing on the edge banding. Measure and cut strips of adhesive-backed wood-veneer banding to fit each of the exposed edges you sanded in Step 6. One strip at a time, hold the veneer — adhesive side down — against an exposed wood edge; press the strip firmly with a preheated iron until the veneer adheres. Use the iron's tip to press the banding down along a curve (*above*).

11 Trimming the banding. Hold a wood shaver at a slight angle to the edge of the banding and lightly scrape off any overhanging, excess veneer by pulling the shaver toward you in long, even strokes. Do not scrape too hard, lest you gouge the wood. Then sand the trimmed edges smooth; take care not to sand the face of the banding, or else you will mar its surface.

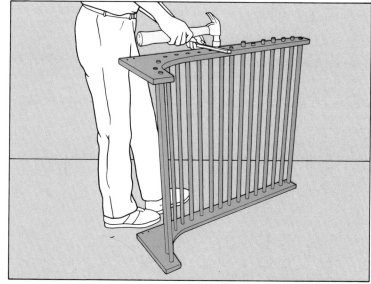

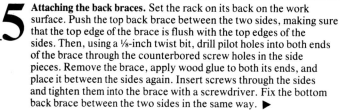

14 Setting the tight dowels. Put the rack on the side in which you first inserted the dowels. Place a piece of scrap wood across the other side next to any dowel you were unable to push all the way through the hole. Tap on the scrap wood with a hammer until the dowel begins to protrude. Work your way along the side until every dowel extends at least ½ inch from its hole.

15 Attaching the back braces. Set the rack on its back on the work surface. Push the top back brace between the two sides, making sure that the top edge of the brace is flush with the top edges of the sides. Then, using a ⅛-inch twist bit, drill pilot holes into both ends of the brace through the counterbored screw holes in the side pieces. Remove the brace, apply wood glue to both its ends, and place it between the sides again. Insert screws through the sides and tighten them into the brace with a screwdriver. Fix the bottom back brace between the two sides in the same way. ▶

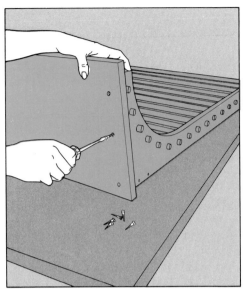

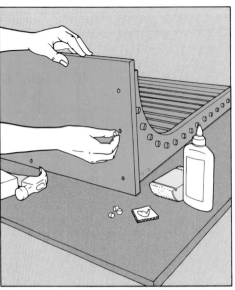

16 **Attaching the top shelf.** With the nearly finished rack on its back, position the shelf at the tops of the sides so that it extends 1 inch beyond each side. Hold the shelf in place and, using the ⅛-inch bit, drill pilot holes through the counterbored screw holes into the tops of the sides and back brace. Remove the shelf and apply glue to the top of the sides and back brace. Put the shelf back, insert the screws, and tighten them.

17 **Inserting wood plugs.** Squeeze a little glue onto a piece of cardboard. Dip one end of a wood plug into the glue, then insert it into one of the counterbored screw holes. Press the plug into place; if necessary, hammer lightly on a piece of scrap wood held against the plug. Immediately wipe off any excess glue with a damp cloth. Plug the other holes, and sand the tops of the plugs to make them flush with the surrounding surface.

18 **Completing the rack.** Make the final adjustment of the dowels by pushing and twisting them, tapping on scrap wood held to their ends if necessary. They should extend about ½ inch from each side. Finish the rack with a wood stain, following the manufacturer's directions.

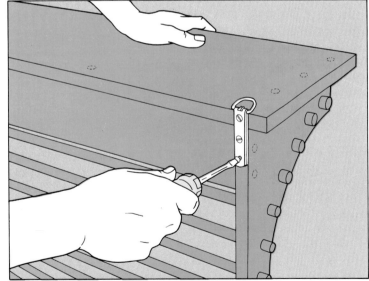

19 **Attaching the hanger strips.** Position one of the heavy-duty mirror hangers along the right back edge of the top and side pieces so that the hanger loop extends above the top of the shelf. Make pencil marks through the holes in the hanger strip and onto the wood. Do the same thing on the other end of the rack. Next, drill holes into the rack at the screw-hole marks, using the ⅛-inch bit. Hold the hangers in position as you screw them into place. If you are attaching the rack to a wall that has studs, make sure that at least one hanger will be screwed into a stud. To do this, you may have to add a third hanger to the back of the rack.

20 **Fastening the rack to a masonry wall.** While a helper holds the rack against the wall, lay a carpenter's level on the top shelf and adjust the rack so that it is straight; then draw a pencil mark through the hanger loop and onto the wall. Remove the rack and — wearing safety goggles — drill into the wall, using a ⁵⁄₁₆-inch masonry bit. Insert 1½-inch lead anchors (*page 39*) into the holes, tapping them in with a hammer if necessary. Have your helper hold the rack in position; insert a 1½-inch pan-head sheet-metal screw and a flat washer through the hanger loop and into the lead anchors. Tighten the screws, making sure that the washer grips the hanger loop as the screw fits into place.

An overhead pot rack

The gleaming steel pot rack shown at right frees precious shelf space while providing instant access to everyday cookware. Its bare bolts and chains complement the designs of pots, bringing them out of the cupboard to display them in full view.

All this can be achieved quite simply, because most of the parts are available from a hardware store. The rack's corner brackets are predrilled, and a hardware dealer generally will cut to length the four chains that suspend the rack. The strips that form the frame are made of ⅛-inch-thick mild steel, a metal soft enough to be sawed to length by hand, although a steel distributor or an ironworks shop can do the job for you with a special power saw.

Pot hooks can be bought from kitchenware or restaurant-supply dealers or made at home from metal rods *(page 45)*. The only remaining jobs are putting holes in the strips with a power drill and filing down rough edges.

Making this rack calls for six common tools: a hacksaw, a flat metalworking file, a hardened-steel center punch, a ball-peen hammer, a power drill and a small cylindrical — or rattail — metalworking file. The hacksaw will cut quickly through mild steel; an inexpensive hardened-steel blade with 18 teeth per inch is ideal for this job, but a finer or coarser blade will do, provided it is sharp. A flat file about 10 inches long is then used to smooth the sawed ends *(Step 2);* a double-cut file (one with crisscrossing gullets that create a fast-cutting diamond pattern) is best, but any flat file will suffice.

Drilling holes in mild steel requires a hardened-steel center punch (similar to a woodworker's awl), which is struck with a hammer to make a sharp dent that starts the drill bit. For this task, the classic metalworking hammer is the ball-peen type. This hammer has a broad striking face — called the poll — that precludes glancing blows; an ordinary claw hammer, however, does almost as well. The basic design and metallurgical properties of the two hammers are identical.

The hole is bored with a power drill fitted with a ⅜-inch twist bit, the all-purpose type common in woodworking *(page 125)*. To remove burrs from the hole, choose a small, cylindrical metalworking file, often called a rattail file.

After the rack is bolted together, the cold-rolled steel should be scrubbed with an alcohol-soaked rag to remove any grease. The rack then is sealed against rust — either with automobile wax, which requires annual renewing, or with polyurethane varnish, which is longer-lasting but so brittle that pots may chip it.

The best location for the rack is at least 4 feet above an island of cabinets or a counter that abuts a window or a blank wall. There, dangling pots will not attract grease from the stove, block shelves and cabinet doors, or bruise the cook's head. To have the chains vertical, the rack's outside dimensions — 16 inches by 32 inches — are designed to align its corners with ceiling joists spaced the usual 16 inches apart. By keeping the dimensions in multiples of 16 inches, you can build a larger rack that will hang similarly.

Materials List	
Steel strip	1¼″ x ⅛″ cold-rolled mild-steel strip, 8′ long, cut into: 2 side pieces, 32″ long 2 end pieces, 16″ long
Angle brackets	4 1¼″ x ⅛″ predrilled cold-rolled mild-steel angle brackets, 8″ long
Bolts	24 5/16″ machine bolts, ¾″ long, with matching flat washers and nuts
Screw eyes	4 ¼″ screw eyes, 2″ long
S hooks	8 zinc-plated S hooks, 2″ long
Chain	welded, zinc-plated 3/16″ chain, cut into 4 equal pieces, length determined by ceiling height
Finish	automobile wax

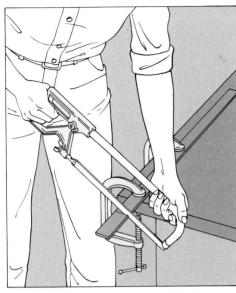

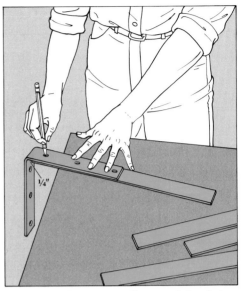

1 **Cutting a steel strip.** Measure 32 inches from one end of a strip of 1¼-by-⅛-inch cold-rolled mild steel; draw a line squarely across it. Secure the strip along a worktable edge with two C clamps. Set a hacksaw's blade on the line and repeatedly draw the saw back to cut a groove. Then put your free hand on the hacksaw frame. Saw with long, slow strokes, using both hands to press down firmly on the forward stroke but applying no pressure on the return stroke.

2 **Filing the end.** Set a metalworking file at right angles to the cut end of the strip and diagonally across it, holding the handle in one hand and the tip in the other. In smooth, rhythmic strokes, slide the file downward with moderate pressure and lift it away while you pull it back. File the end only until all metal burrs and sharp edges are gone; it need not be perfectly smooth. Cut and file a second 32-inch strip and two 16-inch strips.

3 **Marking screw holes.** Set an angle bracket over the end of one strip, with the bracket's corner ¼ inch beyond the end of the strip, and mark circles through the bracket's holes onto the metal strip. Mark both ends of each strip in the same way.

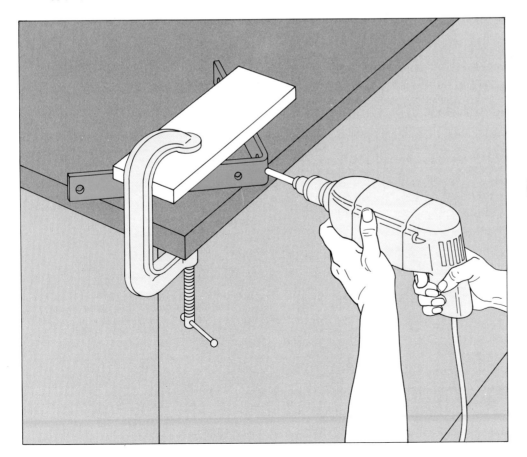

6 **Drilling the brackets.** To make a hole for each corner's supporting chain, clamp the angle bracket between a scrap of wood and the worktable. Center-punch for a single hole at the outside of the corner *(Step 4)*, then enlarge the dent by hand *(Step 5)* and slowly drill through the strip with a ⅜-inch twist bit, bisecting the right angle between the bracket's arms. Drill the other brackets in the same way, then smooth the holes with a rattail file.

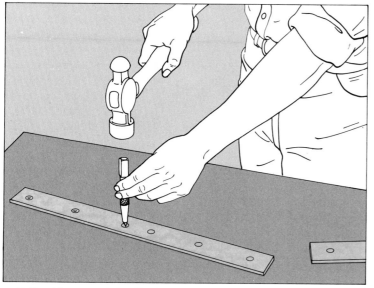

4 **Punching starter holes.** Set the point of a center punch at the center of each marked screw hole. Hold the punch vertical and make a small dent in the strip by tapping the punch's head once or twice with a ball-peen hammer or, lacking that, with a claw hammer.

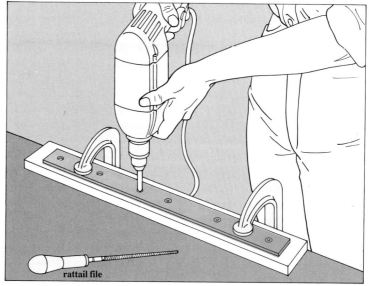

rattail file

5 **Drilling the strips.** Clamp a steel strip to the worktable atop some scrap wood, and fit a power drill with a ⅜-inch twist bit. Set the bit in the punched dent, press lightly and turn the drill chuck by hand to enlarge the dent slightly. Wearing safety goggles, start the drill and apply steady, firm pressure with both hands; if your drill has a variable speed control, set it at slow speed. Stop drilling for a few minutes at any hint of blackening or smoke. As the bit reaches the strip's bottom, press very lightly and hold the drill tightly to prevent binding.

Drill the other holes similarly, then file away metal flakes and burrs by sliding a small rattail file through each hole.

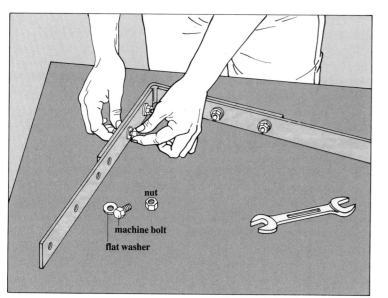

nut

machine bolt

flat washer

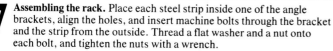

7 **Assembling the rack.** Place each steel strip inside one of the angle brackets, align the holes, and insert machine bolts through the bracket and the strip from the outside. Thread a flat washer and a nut onto each bolt, and tighten the nuts with a wrench.

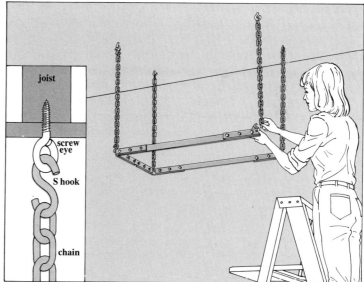

joist

screw eye

S hook

chain

8 **Hanging the rack.** Finish the rack by sealing it with automobile wax, then locate the ceiling joists above its planned location *(page 36)*. At one joist, mark points 16 inches apart for the rack's end or 32 inches apart for its side. With your helper, hold the rack's corners against the marks, mark the other two corners on the ceiling and make sure these marks are centered on a joist; move them if necessary.

At each mark, drill a ³⁄₁₆-inch pilot hole straight up into the joist and install a screw eye *(page 40);* slip an S hook and a precut length of chain onto each screw eye *(inset, above).* Slide S hooks into the holes at each corner of the rack; then, with a helper, slip the upper end of each hook onto the chain dangling from a matching screw eye.

A guide
to new cabinets

The profusion of kitchen cabinet designs and styles belies the fact that basically these units are just rectangular boxes. The cabinets may hold shelves or drawers, an oven or a sink, even a pop-up dining table or telescoping ironing board; their proportions may change dramatically as their roles shift. But behind their façades of Colonial scallops or Art Deco ziggurats, cabinets remain rectangles — and this consistency of outline makes cabinets easy to arrange in attractive layouts *(pages 68-69)* that suit endlessly varied individual needs.

If the time has come to replace the cabinets in your kitchen, you can sketch out your ideas, then have a local cabinetmaker build and install the units. You can order custom cabinets — imported or American-made — that can be modified to fit your requirements with such niceties as cutlery drawers lined in tarnish-resistant cloth. The importers and distributors of such wares will see to their installation. More affordable — and more susceptible of amateur installation *(pages 64-65)* — are the stock cabinets sold at department stores, manufacturer's showrooms, lumberyards and home centers. The lowest in cost are sold unfinished and, sometimes, in sections for assembly. Stock units come in standard dimensions, but other sizes can be specially ordered.

In all systems, base units are 24 inches from back to front and 34½ inches high. A conventional plastic-covered plywood countertop is 1½ inches high; it brings the height of base cabinets level with a 36-inch stovetop. The countertop itself must be built separately *(pages 82-83)*.

The potential width of base units ranges from 9 to 60 inches, in increments of 3 inches. No single cabinet, of course, is sold in so many sizes. The single-door cabinet at the beginning of the second row here, for example, comes as narrow as 9 inches, as wide as 24 inches. The drawer unit below it varies from 12 to 24 inches.

Wall units are usually 12 inches front to back and may be 12 to 30 inches high; typically, the shorter cabinets are used above refrigerators. In width, the units range from 12 to 60 inches, in 3-inch increments. Special-use cabinets to hold cleaning supplies or support a wall oven are 24 inches deep and reach 84 inches high; widths vary.

Because few kitchen walls are multiples of 3 inches and are perfect verticals meeting at true right-angled corners, cabinet manufacturers supply so-called filler strips: sections of matching cabinet front that fill gaps where combi-nations of units do not exactly fit a wall. Strips come in the same heights as wall and base cabinets and in widths of 3 or 6 inches; they are available flat and as right angles. Wood fillers can be sawed to narrower dimensions.

Steel cabinets are prized for strength and durability; a baked-on enamel finish makes them virtually impervious to moisture and stains. However, if you want steel cabinets, you will have to have them professionally installed. All of the cabinets sold for amateur installation are wood.

Solid wood and furniture-grade plywood are generally favored for the parts of a cabinet that are constantly on view: the front of the frame, the doors, the drawer fronts. Even in costly units, the body of the cabinet, the shelves and the drawers are likely to be made of utilitarian plywood or of hardboard (a sheet of compressed wood fibers) or particleboard (coarse wood particles compressed with glue into a sheet). Identifying materials may not be easy: Hardboard can be made with a wood-grain pattern, and particleboard can be covered with wood veneer or with a plastic laminate that looks like wood.

With so many combinations of materials possible, your best assurance of quality cabinets is to visit as many dealers as time allows, taking notes and collecting all the catalogues and price lists you can. Bring a tape measure with you: Shelves, whether plywood or particleboard, should be at least ¾ inch thick to bear the loads that kettles or canned goods might put on them. Doors, too, unless they are steel, should be at least ¾ inch thick for sturdiness and smooth swinging.

Inspect cabinets to see that surfaces are smooth and edges straight, that doors hang true and hinges fit snugly. Press down on shelves to determine whether they will give or hold their place. Open doors and slam them shut to test the responsiveness of hinges and catches; slide drawers in and out to see how they ride in their channels.

Cabinets that meet your standards of performance will also be available in a variety of finishes. Be sure you pick one that will stand up: polyurethane varnish, alkyd paint, or plastic laminate. General practice is to finish only the fronts of cabinets, but you can also order matching finish for one or both sides or for the backs if these surfaces will be visible once the cabinets have been installed. Similarly, you can order doors hinged on either the right or the left — whatever will best suit your kitchen and make your new cabinets most useful and enjoyable.

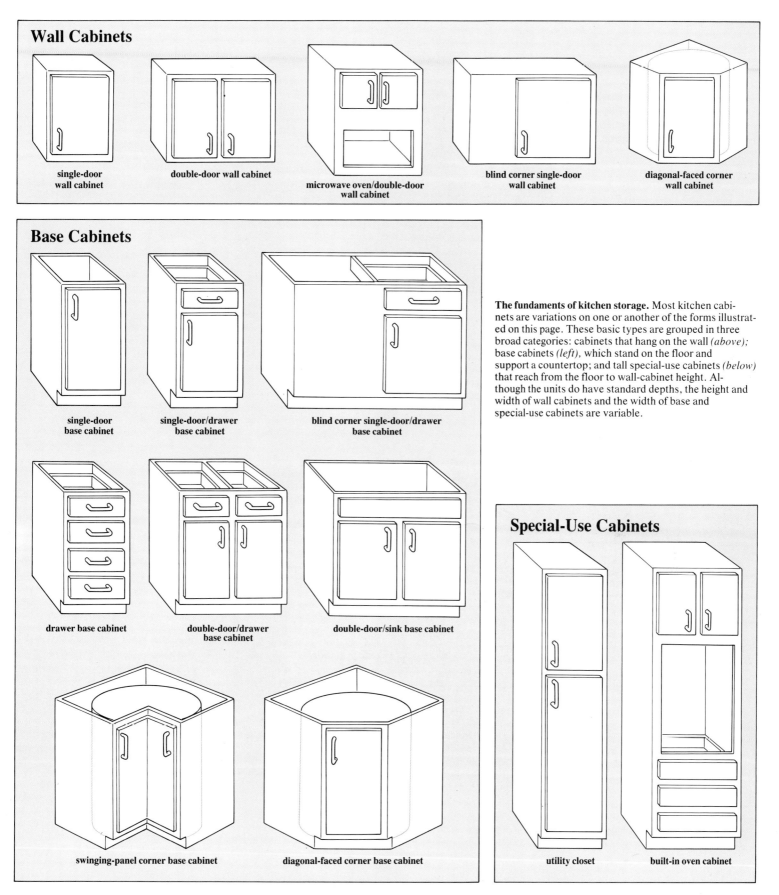

Wall Cabinets

single-door
wall cabinet

double-door wall cabinet

microwave oven/double-door
wall cabinet

blind corner single-door
wall cabinet

diagonal-faced corner
wall cabinet

Base Cabinets

single-door
base cabinet

single-door/drawer
base cabinet

blind corner single-door/drawer
base cabinet

drawer base cabinet

double-door/drawer
base cabinet

double-door/sink base cabinet

swinging-panel corner base cabinet

diagonal-faced corner base cabinet

The fundaments of kitchen storage. Most kitchen cabinets are variations on one or another of the forms illustrated on this page. These basic types are grouped in three broad categories: cabinets that hang on the wall *(above)*; base cabinets *(left)*, which stand on the floor and support a countertop; and tall special-use cabinets *(below)* that reach from the floor to wall-cabinet height. Although the units do have standard depths, the height and width of wall cabinets and the width of base and special-use cabinets are variable.

Special-Use Cabinets

utility closet

built-in oven cabinet

Corner Configurations

If two runs of cabinets are to meet in a corner of your kitchen, start your planning at that junction and work outward along the walls from there. The corner calls for special handling, as the drawings here illustrate, and how you decide to deal with it will affect all the rest of your cabinet layout.

The dead-corner treatment, in which ordinary cabinets are joined by a filler strip *(below, left)*, is by far the least ex-pensive arrangement. But it wastes so much potential storage space that it may well not be the most economical layout, especially if your kitchen is small.

Substituting a blind cabinet for one of two ordinary wall or base units *(below, center)* fills the corner space, providing a compromise between cost and utility. However, the most appealing, though also most expensive, option is corner cabinets such as those at right, below.

They offer a maximum of usable storage space — generally on shelves that revolve like a lazy susan.

For symmetry, of course, the wall and base units should harmonize. In both the dead-corner and blind-cabinet layouts, cabinets meet at right angles so these can be mixed or matched as you like. Diagonal-faced corner cabinets, by contrast, must always be paired with each other to look their best.

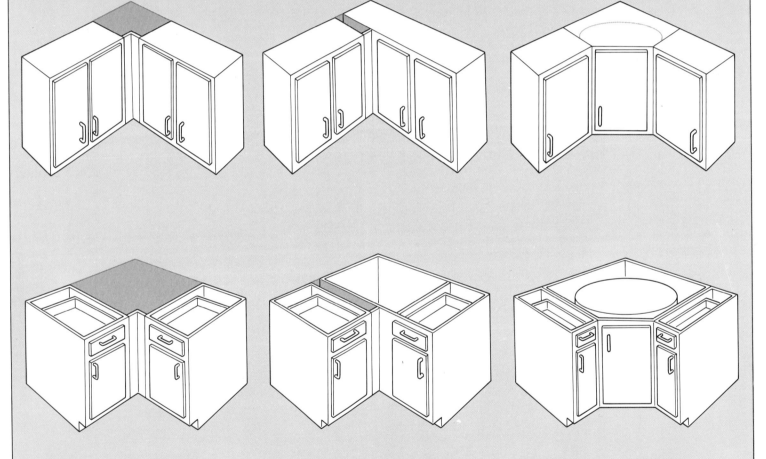

A dead corner. Whether you are dealing with wall units *(top)* or base units *(bottom),* the simplest and cheapest way to treat a corner is to link the two cabinet runs with an L-shaped corner filler. The filler strip's 3-inch legs give drawers and doors room to open. Because the filler substitutes for a corner cabinet, the cost saving is substantial. But so is the loss of storage space — up to 4 cubic feet behind wall cabinets, 15 cubic feet behind base cabinets.

Reach-in storage. Blind corner cabinets — wide units that are doorless on one side — are a common solution to the corner problem. A flat filler strip 3 inches wide *(at left on the pairs of cabinets above)* assures leeway for opening doors or drawers. The problem is self-evident: You must reach deep inside to gain access to the concealed shelves. An item that gets shoved far back into a blind cabinet may not be seen again until spring-cleaning time.

Revolving shelves. The most rewarding — and most expensive — way to turn a corner is with cabinets that hold a lazy susan behind a diagonal face *(above)* or swinging right-angled panels *(page 65, bottom left).* Nothing stored in one of these large units is out of reach for long. Be aware, however, that a base corner cabinet takes 36 inches of wall space on each side, and a wall corner cabinet takes 24 inches.

Plotting a perfect layout

However glamorous new cabinets may appear in a showroom, the acid test is how they look in your kitchen. You can gauge colors by taking home swatches of the possible finishes. But unless the cabinets will be exactly the same sizes as existing ones, you will need scale drawings of the layout you envision in order to judge it in advance.

The first step is to map out floor and wall outlines such as those shown below. With these as your framework, you can plot cabinet layouts accurate to the last detail *(pages 68-69)*. Start by measuring the kitchen area where the cabinets will go, and everything in the area that will affect the cabinet layout. You will need an 8-foot folding ruler or a long steel tape and a helper to accomplish the measuring; the drawings will require graph paper and tracing paper.

First, measure each wall from corner to corner at several heights and from floor to ceiling at two or three points. If the results vary, record the lowest figures; filler strips and shims *(pages 72-73)* will compensate for uneven walls and cabinet combinations that do not quite fill available space. Then measure every architectural obstacle to cabinets — doors, windows, soffits and such — and measure the wall around them to fix their position. For example, measure from a corner to the edge of a window, across the window, then from the other edge to the next corner.

Next, measure every fixture or appliance that will still be there when your new cabinets are installed. If you plan to move any appliance or replace it, use the new location or dimensions for your list of measurements. Stop to see that the total of sequential measurements, such as those across the window wall, matches the overall measurement.

Finally, use the figures to create scale drawings on graph paper of your floor area and each of the walls where you will install cabinets. Whether each square of the graph paper represents 1 inch, 2 inches or — as in the drawings below — 3 inches is up to you. But keep the scale large so that your drawings can reflect details clearly. Round off measurements to whole numbers for drawing layouts, but record all of the key dimensions — including fractions — either on the layouts or on the page beside them.

At this stage, you are ready to sketch in whatever cabinet layouts you fancy. Place tracing paper over your floor plan, and plot the base cabinets first. Start with a corner, and work along the adjacent walls to the end or the next corner. Bear in mind your needs for point-of-first-use storage at each work center *(pages 18-19)*.

Always try to choose the widest suitable cabinets: One large unit costs less than two small ones and is easier to install. If the space from a corner cabinet to an appliance is 53 inches, for instance, the largest single unit you could use would be a 51-inch one. (Divide the total measure by 3, which is the width increment for cabinets; subtract the remainder from the measure to find the maximum usable width.) You might choose a single 51-inch cabinet with three or four doors, or a 36-inch cabinet with two doors plus a 15-inch-wide stack of drawers, or a 27-inch cabinet with one door plus two 24-inch drawer units.

As you proceed to line up the cabinets, indicate where

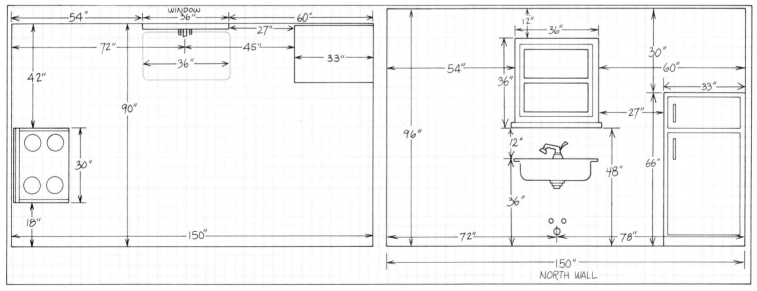

Making a preliminary floor plan. Determine the length of each wall on which you will install cabinets, measuring it first in its entirety, then piecemeal to find the size and position of everything that will affect cabinet placement. Here, for instance, you must know the width of the stove and exactly where along the left-hand wall it stands. You also need to know the location of the sink's plumbing as well as of the sink itself. When you have all the measurements, plot these basic elements of the room on graph paper, drawing them in scale to one another. In this case, one square equals 3 inches — the basic kitchen-cabinet module.

Drawing the walls to scale. For an elevation of each wall of cabinets, take the floor-to-ceiling measurement and such other critical vertical dimensions as the position of the window and sink and the height of the refrigerator. Combine these vertical measurements with the appropriate horizontal measurements you made for the floor plan to plot the dimensions of each wall onto graph paper, using the same scale for the elevations that you used for the floor plan.

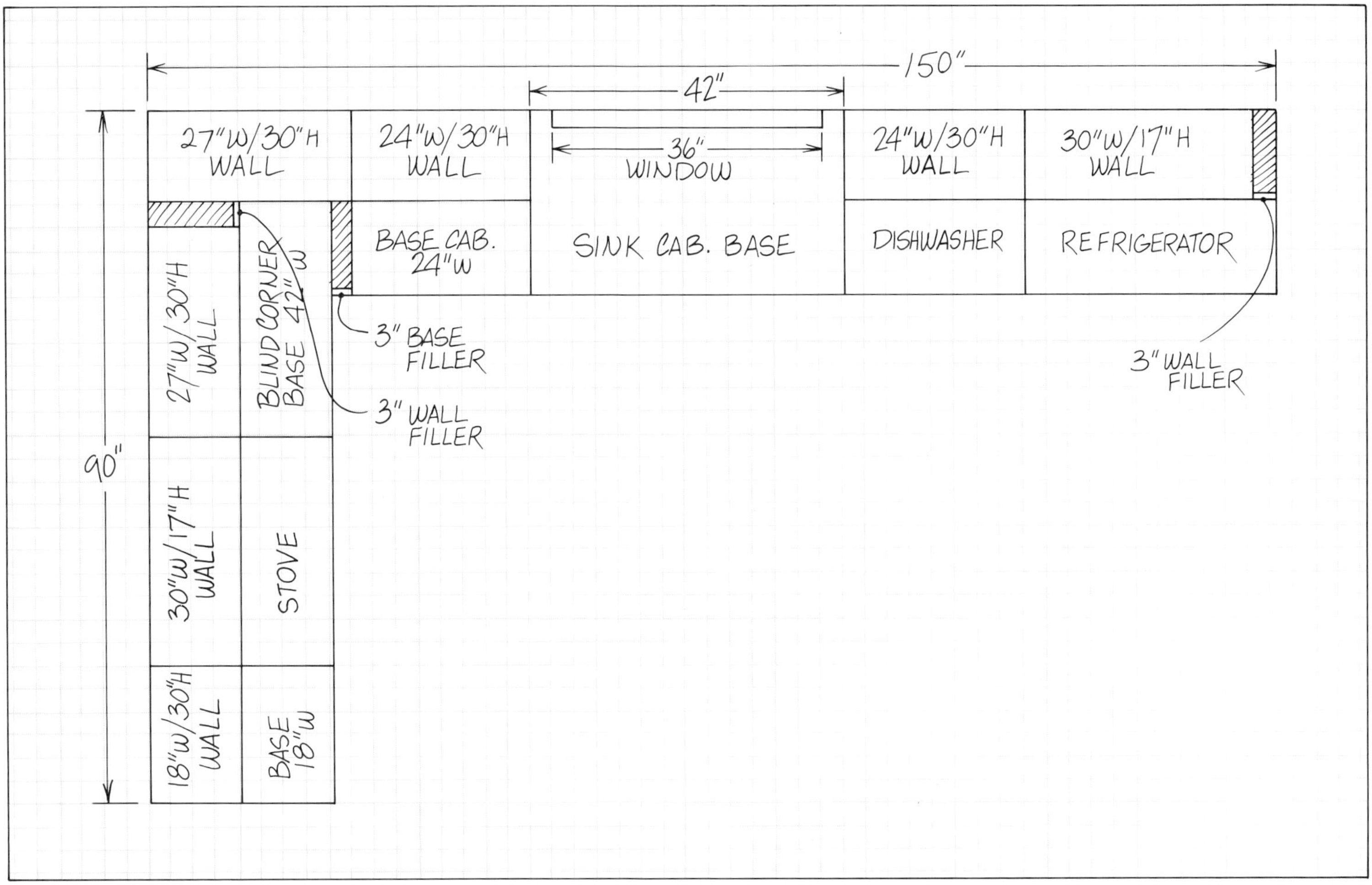

A final floor plan. Place tracing paper on the drawing of the floor without cabinets *(page 67)*, and experiment with arrangements of various cabinet sizes and types on the tracing paper until you find one you like. Using the same scale as in earlier drawings, first plan the arrangement of base units, working out from the corner, the most difficult section *(page 66)*. Use other sheets of tracing paper to plot the wall units. Draw in wall and base fillers where you will need to use them. Then take a fresh piece of graph paper to draw the room again and to combine the arrangements for the base and wall units. Record the width of all cabinets — and the height of any wall units — on the plan.

fillers will be needed and how wide these will be. If you are working with a catalogue, make a note of order numbers of each cabinet you choose; otherwise, keep notes on the specific features you expect each cabinet to have, and whether doors are hinged on the right or the left side. Either way, write the required dimensions on the plan.

When you have completed the base runs, put another sheet of tracing paper on top of both the graph-paper plan and the tracing-paper layout of base cabinets, and work out a scheme for the wall cabinets. Again, usability is the most important criterion, but for appearances' sake you will want the outer edges of the runs to coincide.

Finally, use fresh paper to draw views, such as those shown at right, of the walls where the cabinets will be installed. The base cabinets themselves will be 34½ inches tall; standard countertops will add 1½ inches, so sketch bases with a total height of 36 inches. If you want to raise or lower the cabinets *(page 75)*, show them at their intended total height. This is also the time to decide how much space you will leave between the counter and the wall cabinets.

With your drawings in front of you, ordering cabinets should prove a simple affair. Keep the drawings handy then so you can check the order without opening cartons after the units are delivered, and use the measurements for marking walls when you begin installing the cabinets.

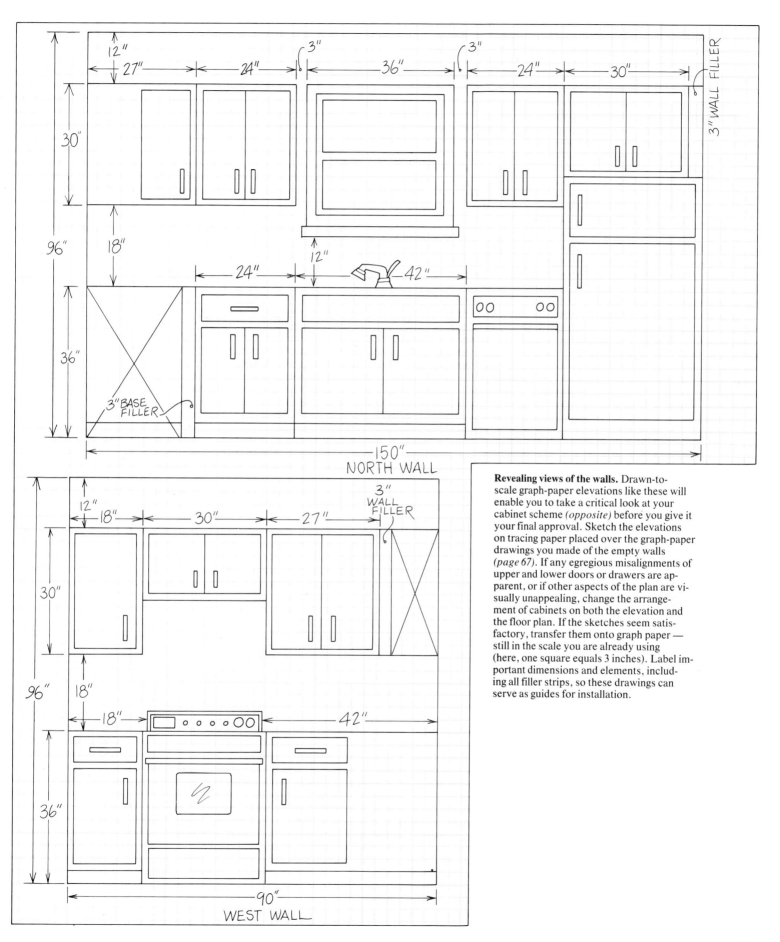

Revealing views of the walls. Drawn-to-scale graph-paper elevations like these will enable you to take a critical look at your cabinet scheme *(opposite)* before you give it your final approval. Sketch the elevations on tracing paper placed over the graph-paper drawings you made of the empty walls *(page 67)*. If any egregious misalignments of upper and lower doors or drawers are apparent, or if other aspects of the plan are visually unappealing, change the arrangement of cabinets on both the elevation and the floor plan. If the sketches seem satisfactory, transfer them onto graph paper — still in the scale you are already using (here, one square equals 3 inches). Label important dimensions and elements, including all filler strips, so these drawings can serve as guides for installation.

Installing base units

Installing stock base cabinets *(below)* requires that you make meticulous measurements ahead of time to ensure a snug fit *(pages 64-69)*. But then — if the way is clear — you need only locate the wall studs, position the cabinets and level them, secure the units to the studs and to each other, and put on a ready-made counter. Even the tool list is a short one: steel tape measure, power drill, screwdriver, hammer, carpenter's level, handsaw and perhaps a carpenter's square.

Not all cabinets are meant to be installed by homeowners. Most custom cabinetry, whether made in America or in Europe, is sold with a warranty conditional on having the maker or dealer install it. For such units, installation often depends on attaching a grooved mounting bar to the wall, then fitting complementary grooves on the backs of cabinets over the bar. You can remove the hanging cabinets by simply lifting them away — an advantage if you move frequently. Stock cabinets are sold like furniture and are permanently attached to the walls, by either the dealer or the buyer, with the techniques shown here.

When you are putting base cabinets against bare walls, start by drawing stud lines *(Step 4)*. If there is a baseboard or other molding on the walls, use a pry bar to pull it off, starting at one end. Later you can cut the molding and renail it to the part of the wall not covered by your new cabinets. If you are putting in new wall cabinets as well as base cabinets, install the wall cabinets first *(page 76)*.

When replacing old cabinets you will need to first empty them, take out the drawers and any loose shelves, and unscrew and lift off the existing counter. You can leave any freestanding appliance, such as stove or refrigerator, in place and functional; however, structurally integrated sinks or appliances must be disconnected by the appropriate experts — the plumber, the electrician, the gas representative.

Before installing the new cabinets, remove the drawers, any loose shelves, and the doors (unscrewing the hinges from the frame) so they will not get in your way. As you proceed, label all doors and drawers, so they can be returned to their original locations after the cabinets are in place.

Putting in new cabinets provides a rare opportunity to position counters at your own best working height if a standard 36-inch counter is too high or too low *(page 75)*. To make the new cabinets level, even if your floor is not, you will need shims — either tapered cedar shingles, available in packages at a lumberyard, or thin pieces of scrap wood — to slip underneath the front of the units and between the cabinets and the walls.

Where the walls are wood-frame, each unit should be attached with wood screws to two studs. If only one stud is located behind a cabinet, use a toggle bolt *(page 41)* as an additional fastener. Where the walls are brick or some other type of masonry construction, consult pages 36-41 to determine the appropriate fasteners and how to use them.

For the finishing touch, nail 1-inch quarter-round molding at the base and sides of the cabinets to cover any gaps at the floor or wall created by shimming the units. Seal the seam between the backsplash and the wall with a bead of latex caulking, then call in the experts to reinstall your sink and appliances.

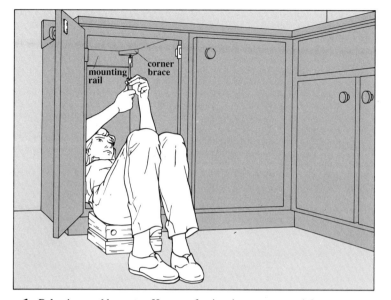

1 **Releasing an old counter.** Have professionals remove any sink or appliance, such as a rangetop, that is installed in the old counter. Lift out the drawers, and store them away from the work area. Then detach the counter by removing the screws from each of the four corner braces inside the top of every old cabinet.

TIP: To avoid stripping the screwhead, match the size of the screwdriver blade to the size of the groove in the screws.

2 **Removing the old counter.** With the aid of a helper, lift the counter off the cabinets and remove it from the work area. If the counter will not budge, it probably has been anchored to the cabinets with glue as well as screws. In that case, insert the tip of a pry bar between the counter and the cabinet below, tapping the pry bar in with a ball-peen hammer, if necessary. Working your way along the cabinets, pry the counter up a little at a time until it can be lifted free.

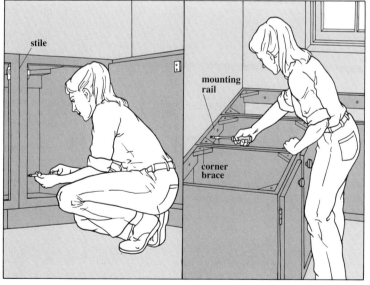

3 **Detaching the cabinets.** Remove the screws from the side edges of the stiles — the vertical members of the front frame of a cabinet *(above, left)*; these screws are the ones that fasten adjacent units to each other or to filler strips. Then remove the screws and any other fasteners, such as toggle bolts, that hold each mounting rail — the board at the upper back of a cabinet — to the wall *(above, right)*. Slide the cabinets away from the wall and remove them from the work area.

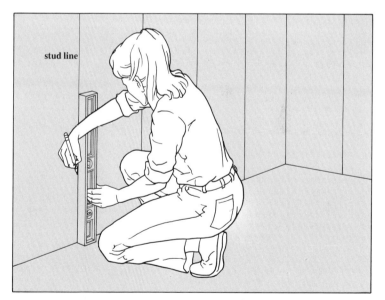

4 **Marking the studs.** Hold a carpenter's level vertically on the wall beside one old mounting-rail screw hole at a time. When the bubbles in the top and bottom windows of the level are centered — indicating that it is vertical — use the level as a straightedge to draw a line to a height of about 4 feet through each screw hole. If you will be placing the cabinets against a new wall, find the studs as shown on pages 36-37, then draw vertical lines to mark their locations. ▶

5 **Checking the level.** Slide the first cabinet into place at a corner or, if your new cabinets do not go into a corner, at one end of the cabinet run. Rest the level on the front top edge of the cabinet — in this case, a blind corner base cabinet. If the bubble in the middle window of the level is centered, the cabinet is level from side to side; if the bubble is closer to one end of its glass tube, that side of the unit is higher than the other. Now move the level to the top edge of one of the sides to determine if the cabinet is level from front to back.

9 **Attaching a filler strip.** Slide the cabinet that will form the second leg of the corner into the work area. Hold the filler strip called for in your plan (*pages 64-69*) against the side of the cabinet that will fit into the corner. Use the level to make sure the faces of the cabinet's stile and the filler strip are flush. Then clamp the filler in place, using scraps of wood to protect the finish of stile and filler from the jaws of the clamps. While your helper holds the cabinet in place, use an adjustable counterbore bit for No. 8 screws to bore two widely spaced pilot holes through the stile of the cabinet into the filler strip. Drive 2½-inch No. 8 flathead wood screws through the stile into the filler strip.

10 **Joining cabinets at the corner.** Slide the unit with the filler strip into place, butting the edge of the filler strip against the already-installed cabinet. Level the new unit, and screw it to the wall as you did the first one. From the inside of the first cabinet, drill a pair of countersunk pilot holes through its wall and straight into the filler strip (*above*). Take care to position the holes so that the drill bit does not hit the screws that are holding the filler strip to the other unit. Drive screws through the pilot holes.

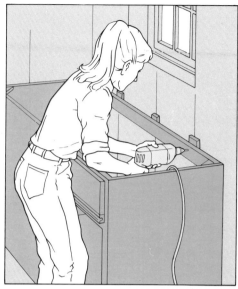

6 **Leveling the unit.** At the lowest corner, tap a shim beneath the cabinet, holding a soft block of wood between the shim and the hammer so the hammer will not scratch the floor. Wedge the shim in just far enough to make the unit level. Then tap additional shims between the cabinet and the floor along the sides and front until the unit is level. Check again with the carpenter's level and readjust the shims if necessary.

7 **Shimming along the wall.** If there is a gap between the back of the leveled cabinet and the wall, slip shims into this space, centering them on the stud lines *(Step 4)*. Tap them in far enough to fit snugly — but not so far that they tip the cabinet. Then check again to make sure the cabinet is still level.

8 **Drilling pilot holes.** Using an adjustable counterbore bit for No. 8 screws, drill countersunk pilot holes through the mounting rail and the shims and at least 1 inch into the studs. Drive 2½-inch No. 8 flat-head wood screws into the holes. Check again with the level; loosen screws and move shims, if necessary, to level the cabinet.

11 **Trimming the shims.** Holding a small saw at an angle and taking care not to scratch the cabinet finish, cut almost all the way through the shims at the bottom of the cabinet. Stop short of the floor, lest you mar its surface. Then snap off the excess pieces of shim. Now use the saw to trim the wall shims at the top of the cabinet, taking the same precautions to protect the wall. ▶

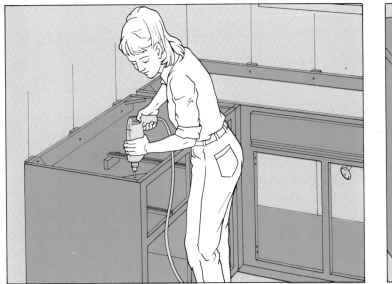

12 **Preparing for the counter.** If the four corner braces at the top of each unit are wood, use a ³/₁₆-inch bit to drill a pilot hole straight down through the center of every one. If the braces are plastic, they will have predrilled pilot holes.

13 **Attaching the counter.** With your helper, lower the counter into place and shove it snug against the walls. Drive No. 10 screws, long enough to reach through the corner brace and halfway through the counter, up into the pilot holes and counter. If the screws lift the counter instead of biting into its underside, have your helper hold the counter down while you drive the screws.
TIP: Because they will not be visible under the braces, round-head screws are good here. They need not be countersunk, and they will bear more weight than flat-head screws in this position.

quarter-round molding

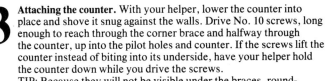

14 **Covering gaps.** Saw strips of 1-inch quarter-round molding several inches longer than each section of cabinets. To start at an inside corner, as shown, use a miter box *(page 29, Step 2)* for cutting off one end of the first strip at a 45° angle from the high edge of the molding inward to the low edge. To start at an outside corner, cut the angle outward.

Set the molding along the toekick — with the angle in the corner — and mark where the cabinets end. If they end at a wall or an appliance, saw straight across the molding at the mark; otherwise, cut a 45° angle. Nail the molding to the floor with finishing nails. Fit another molding strip into the corner, mark and cut it. Nail the second molding strip in place so the ends form a right angle.

Other Common Cabinet Junctions

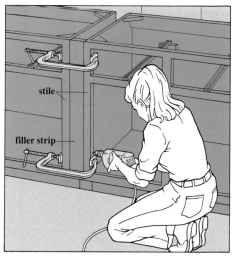

Linking side-by-side units. Attach adjacent cabinets to the wall *(Steps 5-8)*, making sure their faces are flush. Clamp the adjoining stiles together. Then use an adjustable counterbore bit for No. 8 screws to drill two widely spaced, countersunk pilot holes through one stile and ⅝ inch into the other; avoid the door-hinge positions. Drive flat-head No. 8 screws through the holes.

A filler strip in a run. If side-by-side cabinets are to be linked by a filler strip, make sure they are flush before screwing the second cabinet to the wall. Trim the strip to fit the gap; if you are cutting with a circular saw, turn the strip face down so that the saw teeth will not splinter the finished side. Clamp the strip in place as shown above, then attach it with two screws through each of the adjoining stiles *(Step 9)*.

A corner base filler. Once the cabinets are positioned in the corner, set a carpenter's square against the toekicks of the cabinets and measure from the corner of the square to each unit. Mark these distances on a corner base filler. Measure and mark these distances from corner to cabinet near the top and bottom of each unit. Connect the marks with vertical lines; cut the filler with a handsaw. Attach the filler to each adjoining stile with two screws *(Step 9)*.

Adjusting Counter Height

Before you install base cabinets, you can trim their height safely by removing as much as 2 inches from the standard 4-inch toekick with a circular saw. Or you can add up to 4 inches to their height by one or both of the strategies here: installing a wood platform to lift the cabinets from below or attaching boards to the cabinet tops to raise the counter.

After the cabinets are anchored, the visible edge of a platform can be camouflaged with paint or stain matched to the cabinet finish, or it can be hidden by 6-inch vinyl cove molding cemented over the platform and the cabinet's toekick. An extra board atop the cabinets is most easily stained or painted before the counter is set over it. For a total disguise, the board above each cabinet unit can be covered with matching plastic laminate or wood veneer.

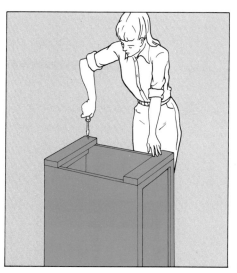

Making a platform. Where the cabinets will stand, butt 2-by-4s together to form a frame with outside dimensions the length and width of the units. Brace the frame with 2-by-4s at 2½-foot intervals before nailing. Set the frame in position and, starting at the lowest corner, level it with shims. Then countersink 3-inch No. 10 flat-head wood screws through the frame into the floor at the corners and through any shims; trim the shims flush. Finally, nail ¾-inch plywood over the frame. Install the cabinets atop the platform.

Lifting the counter. Cut 2-by-4s to the width of a single cabinet or a run of cabinets. With a counterbore bit for a No. 10 screw, drill pilot holes through the 2-by-4s and into the top of each cabinet at the corner braces; then drive 3-inch No. 10 flat-head screws into the braces. Stain, paint or cover the visible edge of the front board before installing the cabinet and screwing the counter on *(Step 13, opposite)*. Use screws long enough to pass through the braces, the 2-by-4s and half the thickness of the counter.

Putting up wall units

Like base cabinets, conventional wall cabinets need only be positioned, leveled and shimmed before being screwed into place. However, to accomplish these jobs while you balance on a ladder, you need a helper to keep the units steady.

The first step in installing wall units is, of course, to clear the wall of shelves, brackets, hooks and such. If there are old wall cabinets, remove them by the techniques you would use for base cabinets — after you have removed any base cabinets (*page 71, Step 3*). This sequence of base cabinets before wall cabinets holds true only in the removal stage: To allow maximum space for ladders, helpers and tools, new wall cabinets should always be installed before new base cabinets are in place.

Start the removal process for the wall cabinets at one end of a run and detach the units individually. Before you begin unscrewing them from each other and from the wall, brace each cabinet in turn by wedging one or two 2-by-4s between the floor and the bottom front edge of the unit. Even with that support, you will need a helper to prevent the cabinets from falling while you take out the last screws.

Once the old cabinets are down, draw the bottom lines for all of the new units onto the wall to ensure that everything will fit according to plan. In most cases, the lines will be 54 inches above the floor to allow 36 inches for the base cabinets and 18 inches between the counter and the wall cabinets.

As you install each of the cabinets, nail up a scrap board, with its top edge set just below the line. Called a cleat, the board will hold the bottom of the back edge of that cabinet in place and level; the cleat can be removed and renailed as you proceed along the wall. It will also provide support during installation, but the cleat cannot take the place of a helper.

Wall cabinets are secured — as comparable base cabinets are — with countersunk flat-head screws driven at least 1 inch deep into the studs of wood-frame walls, with toggle bolts if wood studs are not strategically located, or with masonry fasteners (*pages 36-41*). But wall cabinets have to be fastened in four places: two at the bottom of the unit, two at the top.

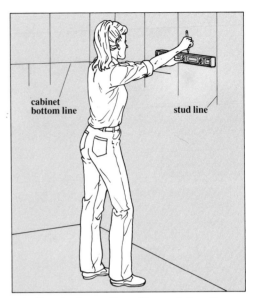

1 **Drawing locator lines.** Clear and clean the walls, then locate the screw holes left in the studs by old cabinets or find the studs (*page 36*). Using a level, draw a vertical line on every stud. Make the lines about 4 feet long, so they will be visible below the cabinet bottom. With your elevations (*pages 64-69*) as a guide, draw a horizontal line to mark the position of each new cabinet.

5 **Hanging adjacent cabinets.** Using a claw hammer, pry the nails from the cleats, then level and nail a cleat to the studs just under the horizontal line for the next cabinet. With your helper, rest the cabinet on the cleat, butting the side of the cabinet against the one you have just installed. Level and shim the cabinet so that its face is flush with that of the first cabinet. Attach the cabinet to the wall as before.

6 **Fastening cabinets together.** Using a C clamp, attach the two stiles of the adjoining cabinets; protect the cabinet finish by placing softwood scraps between the cabinet and the jaws of the clamp. Clamp the cabinets together so that the fronts are flush and gaps are closed, then drill pilot holes with an adjustable counterbore bit, through the stile of the wall cabinet into the adjacent stile of the corner unit. Drive 2¼-inch No. 8 flat-head wood screws into the holes to secure the cabinets together. Saw off the shims with a small saw (*page 73, Step 11*).

2 **Nailing up cleats.** Start the installation of the cabinets at a corner, as shown here, or at the end of the run. Level and then nail boards — in this case, 1-by-3s about 3 feet long — just under the horizontal lines at the corner. Butt the end of one of these cleats against the face of the other where they meet. Nail the cleats directly into the studs, using flat-head nails that protrude a fraction of an inch so they can be easily removed with a claw hammer later.

3 **Positioning a corner cabinet.** Lift the cabinet into the corner, resting it on the cleats. As your helper holds the cabinet up, set the level against the front of the cabinet to be sure it is absolutely vertical. If not, have your helper watch the level while you tap in shims at the stud lines at the back of the cabinet.

4 **Drilling pilot holes.** With your helper still holding the cabinet in place, drill a pair of holes for countersunk screws through each of the mounting rails — the horizontal boards at the top and bottom of the cabinet back — into the studs. Drive 2½-inch No. 8 flat-head wood screws through these holes, two at the top, two at the bottom.

An island that rolls

Mounting kitchen cabinets on wheels rather than walls enables you to create movable storage. If you lay butcher block on top of them, you gain a counter-height work surface that you can use as an island anywhere in the kitchen.

Standard wall cabinets readily adapt to the island design shown at left. Most are about 12 inches deep; fastened back-to-back, they will form a unit 24 inches deep with doors and shelves on both sides.

The cabinets here are 30 inches high; with casters adding 4 inches at bottom and butcher block adding 1¾ inches on top, the island is almost 36 inches tall — average for a counter. But you also can make the height suit your own stature or purpose. A pastry cook, for example, might opt for cabinets 28 inches high with a marble counter 1 inch thick to create a comfortable 33-inch-high work area.

The width of the cabinets can vary to fit your kitchen. The ones here are a generous 42 inches wide; cabinets as small as 18 inches in width would form a stable base. Whatever dimensions you choose, order butcher block or other counter material to overhang the cabinets by 3 inches on every side: The overhang will provide handles when you roll the island.

Finished cabinets are available in a plethora of woods and laminates. Choose units with roofs and bottoms of plywood or particleboard at least ½ inch thick. Most roofs and bottoms will be recessed, and the bottom recess can hold a board to reinforce the base, as in this design.

Unfinished cabinets that you can paint to enliven your kitchen color scheme can be ordered from a cabinet dealer or lumberyard. Specify poplar or birch; either can be readily finished with alkyd primer topped by gloss or semigloss alkyd paint. Avoid oak, which is too porous to produce a smooth painted surface.

The other materials listed at right probably can be found at a hardware store or lumberyard, though for casters you may have to go to an industrial-equipment dealer. Few tools are needed: a power drill, a crosscut or circular saw, a screwdriver, an adjustable wrench, a miter box with a backsaw, and an awl.

Before you begin, remove the cabinet doors to make them less awkward to maneuver. Because the cabinets will be quite heavy once they are bolted together, get a helper to assist in lifting them.

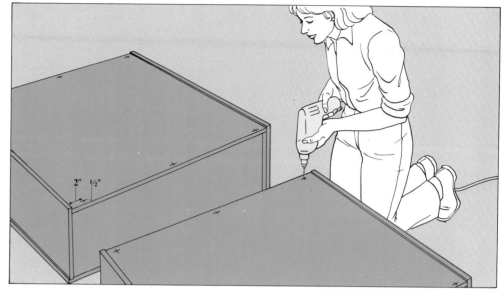

1 **Drilling holes for bolts.** Make a row of three marks ½ inch from the top edge of each cabinet back and a similar row along the bottom edge. For each row, locate the end marks 2 inches from the cabinet sides; locate the third mark midway between the sides. Using a ¼-inch twist bit, drill holes through the backs of the cabinets at all of the marks.

Materials List

Cabinets	2 kitchen wall cabinets, each 42″ x 30″ x 12″
Butcher block	1 piece 1¾″ oak or maple butcher block, 30″ by 48″
Casters	4 locking casters, with wheels 2½″ in diameter, flat steel plates and a rated load capacity of 75 lbs. per caster
1 x 8	1 piece clear pine 1 x 8, 8′ long
Lath	¼″ x 1⅜″ lath, 6′ long
Bolts	6 ¼″ stove bolts, 2″ long, each with a nut and 2 washers
Screws	8 No. 8 round-head wood screws, 1¼″ long 16 No. 8 round-head wood screws, ¾″ long 6 No. 10 round-head wood screws, 3″ long, each with 1 flat washer
Brads	10 No. 18 brads, ¾″ long

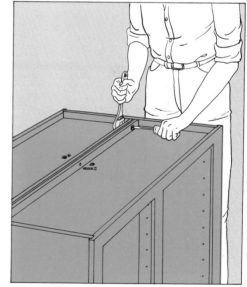

2 **Bolting the cabinets.** Set the cabinets upright and back-to-back. Push an awl through each pair of holes to align them. Slide washers onto three stove bolts; then push the bolts through the holes and slide a second washer and a nut onto each bolt. Tighten each nut with your fingers. Then anchor each bolthead with a screwdriver, fit an adjustable wrench over the nut and push the wrench to tighten the nut. Turn the cabinets over, and bolt the bottom edges together. ▶

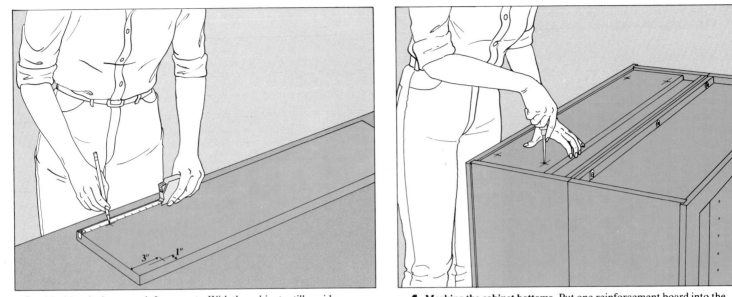

3 **Marking the bottom reinforcements.** With the cabinets still upside down, measure the length of the recessed area in the bottom of one of them. Using a crosscut saw or a circular saw, cut a 1-by-8 into two pieces of that length. Then mark the corners of each board 3 inches from its ends and 1 inch from its sides. Finally, clamp each one to a work-table and use a $\frac{3}{32}$-inch twist bit to drill through the board at every mark.

4 **Marking the cabinet bottoms.** Put one reinforcement board into the recess at the bottom of a cabinet, setting the board snug against the back edge of the cabinet's face. There will be a space several inches wide between the board and the rear of the cabinet. Insert an awl into each corner hole in turn, then push the point firmly into the cabinet bottom. Insert the second board, and mark its location in the other cabinet in the same manner. Remove the boards, and drill a $\frac{3}{16}$-inch hole through the cabinet bottom at each awl mark.

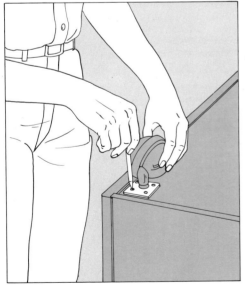

8 **Attaching the casters.** Turn the unit upside down. Set a caster in each corner, with all holes in the plate at least $\frac{1}{2}$ inch from the edges of the reinforcement board. Mark the holes onto the board; with a $\frac{3}{32}$-inch twist bit, drill $\frac{3}{4}$ inch deep at each mark. Place the casters, and drive $\frac{3}{4}$-inch No. 8 round-head wood screws through the holes in the plates and into the boards. Turn the unit over. If the cabinets are unfinished, prime and paint them; finish the lath to match.

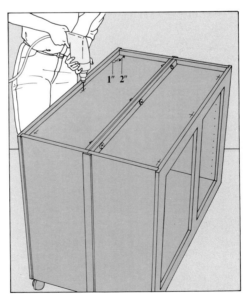

9 **Drilling through the cabinet roofs.** Make a row of three marks 1 inch from the front face on the recessed roof of each cabinet. Locate the end marks 2 inches from the sides, and center the third mark between them. Using a $\frac{1}{4}$-inch twist bit, drill through the cabinet roofs at all of the marks.

10 **Marking the butcher block.** Position the butcher block with its underside up, and draw a straight line 3 inches inside each edge. Cross two pieces of masking tape to mark adjacent corners, aligning the inner edges of the tape with the drawn lines.

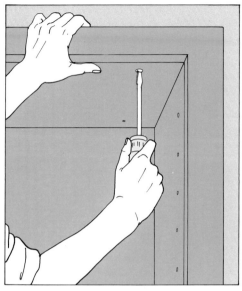

5 **Fastening the boards to the cabinet.** Set the reinforcement boards back in the cabinet bottoms and push the awl through each pair of holes to align them. Clamp the boards to the cabinets beside the center supports *(not shown)*. Then reach inside each cabinet in turn, and drive 1¼-inch No. 8 round-head wood screws up through the cabinet bottoms and into the boards.

6 **Gluing lath over the seams.** Turn the joined cabinets over onto one front face as shown. Cut two 30-inch strips of lath, using a miter box and a backsaw to be sure the ends are square *(page 32, Step 2)*. Squeeze a wavy ribbon of carpenter's glue down the length of each lath piece in turn, and press the lath over one of the seams where the cabinets meet. If glue oozes out, wipe it away with a damp cloth.

7 **Nailing the lath.** Before the glue dries, drive brads 2 inches from both ends of each strip of lath to anchor it. Then drive brads at intervals of 6 or 7 inches into alternate side edges of the strips. Set each brad with a nail set *(page 29, Step 7)*. With a putty knife, spread wood putty over each brad. Lightly scrape away excess putty with the flat edge of the knife and let the putty dry for an hour. Sand the lath smooth, using medium (100-grit) or fine (150-grit) sandpaper.

11 **Anchoring the butcher block.** Set the butcher block atop the cabinets, aligning the taped corners with the corners of the unit. Push an awl up through each hole in the cabinet roofs to mark it on the butcher block *(above)*. Turn the block over, and drill ½-inch-deep holes at each mark, using a ⅛-inch twist bit. Reposition the butcher block. Slip washers onto six 3-inch No. 10 round-head wood screws, and drive the screws up into the block *(right)*. Tighten each screw halfway, then go back and tighten each one completely.

New work surfaces

Like most aspects of kitchen planning, choosing a suitable counter involves a balancing of the various requirements. The ideal counter should be handsome, easy to install, and tough enough to withstand an endless succession of assaults—by water, foods, knife cuts, dropped pots, hot cookware, household chemicals and abrasive cleansers. Not surprisingly, the available materials differ in their virtues, so some compromises may be necessary.

Counters are of two types: integral counters—tough-skinned, factory-built slabs that are fastened directly atop a cabinet; and two-part counters, whose sturdy plywood framework (opposite) is screwed to a cabinet and fitted with a durable countertop material.

Integral counters are simpler to put to work. The dealer will deliver a one-piece counter, ready for installation; the backsplash may be affixed or separate, depending on the counter's material and design. You simply remove the old counter intact (page 71, Steps 1-2) and install the new one (page 74, Steps 12-13). When ordering an integral counter, ask the dealer to come measure your kitchen so you can be sure that all dimensions, including the placement of cutouts for cooktop or sink, are exact. You have a choice of three popular materials:

● *Post-formed laminate counters* have a particleboard base with a rounded front edge and an integral backsplash, all covered at the factory with heat-shaped plastic laminate. They usually are strong and durable, but manufacturing defects may cause weak, chip-prone bonds on curves.

● *Synthetic marble counters,* such as Corian® counters, are made of solid, factory-molded acrylic resin ¾ inch thick; some have precast sinks. Corian counters are cut and shaped with carbide-tipped saw and router blades, either at the factory or at home, and are glued (not screwed) atop a cabinet. Available only in white and shades of beige, this costly material looks much like veined marble, with uniform color throughout its thickness, and weighs almost as much as stone. The surface is susceptible to knife cuts, stains and chipping; it is somewhat heat-resistant, although very hot pots leave irreparable white marks. Minor damage that would permanently mar laminate can be scrubbed away with fine sandpaper or repaired with a plastic filler compound.

● *Butcher-block counters,* made of hardwood strips that are glued together edgewise, can be ordered by the running foot from lumber suppliers, cut to length at the lumberyard or at home, and screwed onto a cabinet. Maple is harder than oak, but both are vulnerable to knife cuts, stains, dents and scorch marks. With age, these expensive counters acquire a handsome patina, but they are not particularly durable; repeated knife cuts splinter the surface, which then must be refinished with a belt sander, and water gradually opens the joints between strips.

Two-part counters are somewhat harder to install but offer a much greater range of decorative possibilities. The countertop material can be custom-fitted to your kitchen, permitting unique edge moldings and backsplash designs. You can even cover the whole backsplash wall with countertop material, an easy-to-clean arrangement favored by many designers.

A new countertop can be installed over old laminate on an existing plywood base, unless the old counter is sagging or badly damaged. Alternatively, you can replace a damaged counter or an old integral counter with a new base, covering the bare plywood with tile or laminate. When ordering materials for a two-part counter, buy everything at once to ensure that colors come from the same dye lot.

As with integral counters, you can choose from among three basic materials:

● *Glazed ceramic tile* is time-consuming to install (pages 84-93). The tiles are embedded in adhesive on bare plywood or on an old laminate-covered counter, and the joints between tiles are filled with colored grout. Tiles are available in many colors, textures and patterns, and can be combined in intriguing geometric patterns. Glazed tile is virtually impossible to scratch or stain, and it is immune to searing temperature. However, tile is so hard that it creates clatter in the kitchen, reflects noise and can break carelessly handled china; and it is so brittle that dropped pots can cause chips or cracks in the tile. It is extremely durable, although the grout tends to absorb stains, and

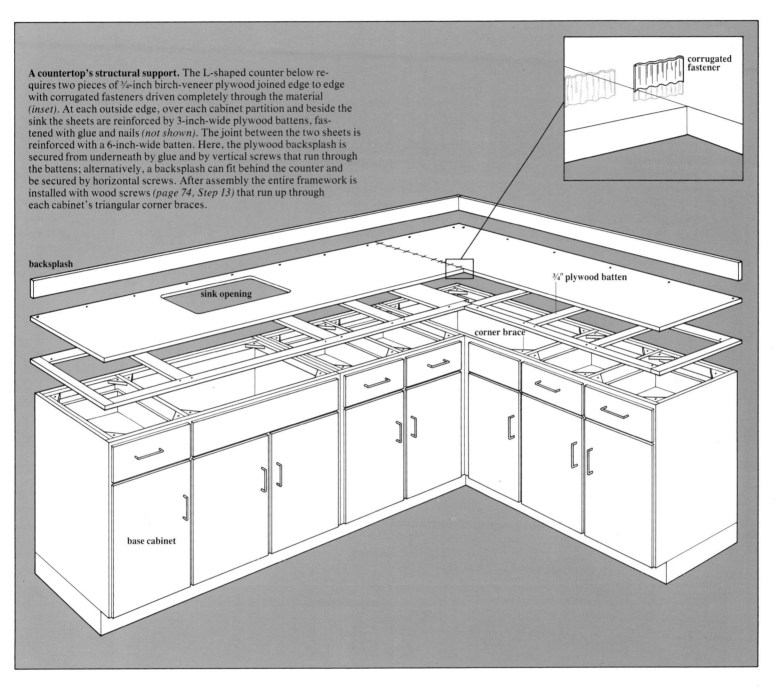

A countertop's structural support. The L-shaped counter below requires two pieces of ¾-inch birch-veneer plywood joined edge to edge with corrugated fasteners driven completely through the material *(inset)*. At each outside edge, over each cabinet partition and beside the sink the sheets are reinforced by 3-inch-wide plywood battens, fastened with glue and nails *(not shown)*. The joint between the two sheets is reinforced with a 6-inch-wide batten. Here, the plywood backsplash is secured from underneath by glue and by vertical screws that run through the battens; alternatively, a backsplash can fit behind the counter and be secured by horizontal screws. After assembly the entire framework is installed with wood screws *(page 74, Step 13)* that run up through each cabinet's triangular corner braces.

corrugated fastener

backsplash

sink opening

¾" plywood batten

corner brace

base cabinet

seeping water can ruin the underlying adhesive bond.
● *Plastic laminate (pages 94-101)* consists of a sandwich of kraft paper that is saturated with strength-giving phenolic resin, covered by decorative paper that is coated with tough, clear melamine resin; all are bonded together under heat and pressure. Usually sold in ¹⁄₁₆-inch sheets, laminate is sawed to size and glued over old laminate, plywood or particleboard, then trimmed with a router. Laminate is available in a dazzling array of colors and textures. The surface is tough but not invulnerable: Knife cuts may expose the unsightly black core; some household chemicals leave stains; sharp impacts can cause cracks or chips; and

hot cookware leaves bubbles or scorch marks. Laminate eventually shows scratch marks from abrasive cleaners, and a piece may come unglued if water seeps under it.
● *Color-cored laminate* such as Colorcore® laminate comes in sheets ¹⁄₂₀ inch thick that are made by much the same process as ordinary laminate but using tinted melamine resin throughout. It is installed in the same way as laminate. As the name implies, the laminate is evenly colored so that edges match the face and scratches are inconspicuous; it is available in a spectrum of hues. In toughness and durability it is virtually identical to ordinary laminate, but it is considerably more expensive.

A ceramic-tile countertop

The essence of tile laying is the fitting of many small pieces into a harmonious whole. That makes covering a counter with glazed ceramic tiles a tedious but artistically rewarding job, whether you are using matching tiles, as shown below, or a combination of colors, textures and designs — or even your own hand-painted tiles *(pages 92-93)*.

Tiles can be laid on any well-braced, level counter, even one already covered with plastic laminate. Because tiny sizes or fancy shapes complicate cutting and fitting tiles, the basic countertop tiles are either 4¼ inches square — known as 4-inch tile — or 6 inches square. The choice is largely esthetic; 4-inch tiles make a small space seem larger and 6-inch tiles do the converse.

To estimate your tile requirements, calculate the area of the counter and backsplash, subtracting for a sink or cooktop. Add a 5 per cent waste allowance, which includes extra tiles that in future years may be needed to replace broken ones. Then divide by the area of a single tile; the result is the number of tiles you need. You will also need L-shaped trim tiles for the counter's edge, mitered or molded corner pieces, and flat tiles with a rounded bullnose edge for the backsplash.

Planning a tile layout is a trial-and-error process governed by three principles: The layout should be symmetrical at the sink and the counter's edges. It should preclude slivers of tile less than 1 inch wide; these are unsightly and hard to cut. Joints between tiles should be kept uniform — either with cross-shaped ceramic spacers, which create ⅛-inch joints, or with a homemade gauge *(Step 3)*.

Once the tiles are successfully laid out in a dry run (without glue), they are bonded to the counter with premixed Type I organic adhesive, or mastic, spread with a notched rectangular trowel. Wet mastic is water-soluble and can be wiped up easily, but the adhesive cures in 24 hours to form a durable, water-resistant bond.

The joints between tiles are filled with grout, the countertop's most vulnerable component. Of the many available colors, dark ones will best hide stains. Easiest to use is latex-based grout made of two components — a cement-based powder and liquid latex. It is applied with a rubber-faced float. After three days, seal the grout with silicone spray, which should be renewed every six months.

To prepare a counter for ceramic tile, have the sink and any appliances removed. If your counter's edge overhangs the base cabinet, you can install trim tiles on the cabinet front (as shown here) after using a circular saw to cut the edge flush with the cabinet. Alternatively, you can make the edge as deep as your trim tile by nailing and gluing a strip of 1- or 2-inch lumber to its underside. Fill any cracks or chips in the old countertop that are larger than a nickel *(box, page 101);* sand the counter with coarse (60-grit) paper to permit a strong adhesive bond.

The tile job will render the sink and counter unusable for about a week, including the curing periods for mastic and grout. When the grout has been sealed, have your plumber install the old sink, or a new one, seating it in a bed of caulk.

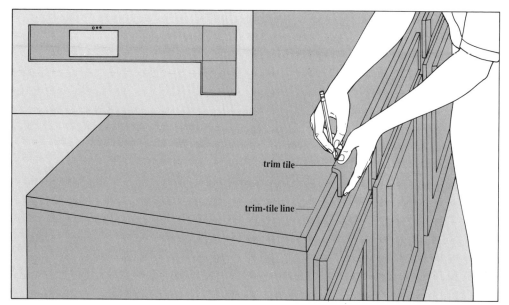

1 **Marking for trim tile.** At one end of the counter, set a trim tile against the edge, with its lip overlapping the counter's top. Hold a pencil against the lip, and slide the tile and pencil together along the edge, drawing a line on the counter. Mark the other edges in the same way. On an L-shaped counter, use a carpenter's square to extend the lines from the L's corner all the way to the walls *(inset).*

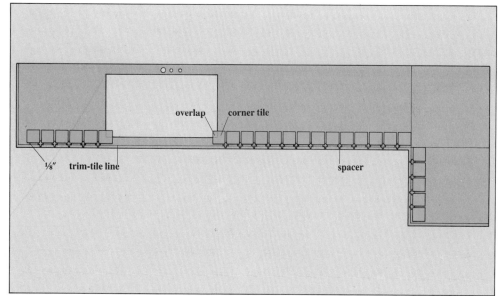

2 **The layout for an L-shaped counter.** On the section of the counter containing the sink, set the first dry tile at the L's corner; use ceramic spacers to place the tile ⅛ inch behind the marked trim-tile line. Align the adjacent side of the tile with the perpendicular line. Working from this tile, lay a row of dry tiles from this corner tile to the sink, and slip ceramic spacers into the joints. Measure the overlap between the last tile and the side of the sink opening, then position a tile with the same overlap on the other side of the sink and continue the tile row to the counter's end. Finally, on the L's other counter, set a matching corner tile; lay tiles and spacers to the end. ▶

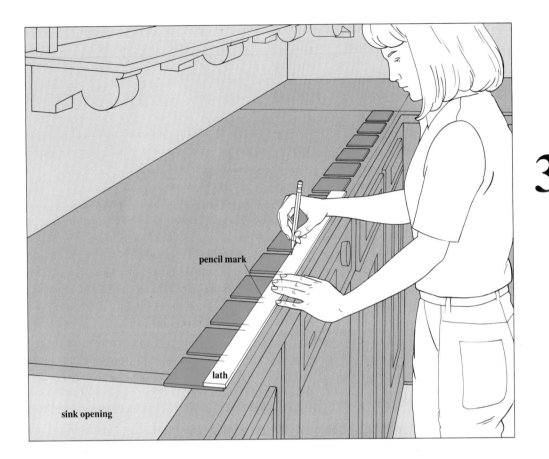

pencil mark

lath

sink opening

3 **Checking the layout.** If the layout shows that tiles beside the sink and at the ends of the counter will be at least 1 inch wide, proceed to Step 4. Otherwise, remove the spacers and make wider, uniform joints between tiles and between the tiles and the trim-tile lines until all end tiles are at least 1 inch wide; the joints should be no wider than 3/16 inch. Then make a joint gauge: Hold a 3-foot length of 1/4-inch lath atop the tile row between the corner and the sink *(left)*, and draw pencil lines on the lath at both edges of each tile.

A Simple Layout for a Straight Counter

If your counter does not have an L, omit Steps 2 and 4. Instead, center a tile on the sink's center line (or, for a counter that does not have a sink, the counter's center line), with its front edge about 1/8 inch behind the line marked in Step 1. Lay a row of dry tiles from this tile across the entire counter front, and slide spacers into the joints.

Check the layout: If the columns of tile at the sink's side or at the end of the counter will be less than 1 inch wide, remove the tiles and redo the layout. First try placing a tile joint on the center mark; if this expedient fails, discard the spacers and make uniform, wider joints between the tiles and between the row and the marked trim-tile line. Check these joints, using a new joint gauge fashioned from lath as in Step 3.

6 **Tracing the tile pattern.** Hold down each tile in turn with one hand, and outline its edges with bold pencil strokes. As you proceed, remove the tile and any spacers around it, and set them aside.

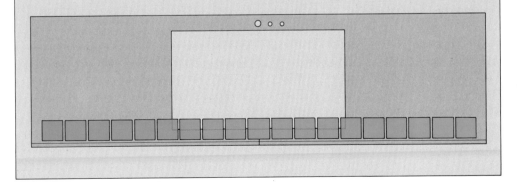

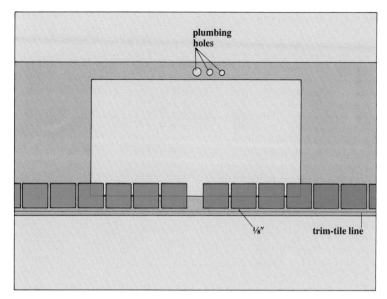

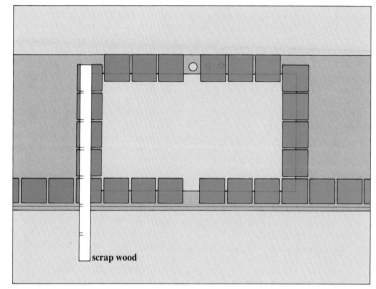

4 **The sink-front layout.** Working from each side of the sink opening, fill in the row of dry tiles until there is not room for a full tile in the center of the row *(above).* Use ceramic spacers — or the joint gauge, if you had to make one — to maintain uniform joint spacing. If the space remaining for the center tile is less than 1 inch wide, remove the tiles from the sink and try to improve the layout. First draw a line to mark the center of the sink opening. Then center a full tile on the mark and complete the row to each side. If this method yields space for tiles less than 1 inch wide at the sink's sides, remove the row of tiles again. Locate a joint on the center line, and work out to the sides.

5 **Layout around the sink.** At each side, remove the tile just outside the one overlapping the sink opening's front corners, and set a carpenter's square against the trim-tile line and the outside edge of the corner tile. Draw a pencil line across the counter, then replace the missing tile. Set a column of dry tiles along each line, using ceramic spacers or the joint gauge *(above)* made in Step 3 for uniform joint spacing. If the gap at each column's end is between ¼ and ¾ inch — requiring a small sliver of tile — repeat Steps 2 through 4 with slightly wider joints, then redo this step with the new spacing. Lay tiles behind the sink only if the rim of counter is at least 1 inch wide; the sink lip will cover a narrower rim. Weight the overhanging tiles with scrap lumber if necessary.

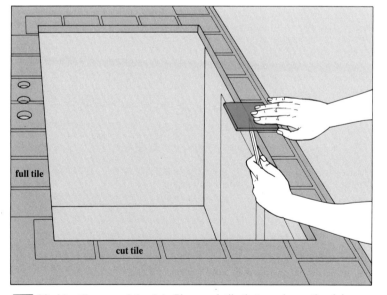

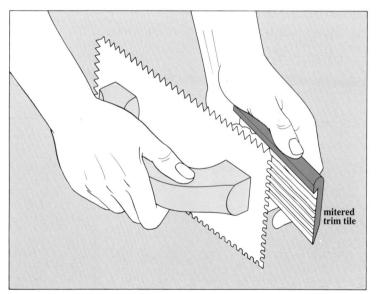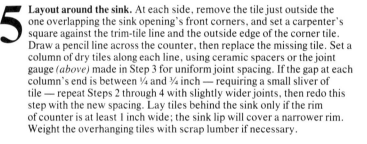

7 **Marking tiles around the sink.** Place each tile that overhangs the sink opening so that it is face down in its penciled outline. Holding the tile in position with one hand, reach into the sink opening and from underneath pencil the opening's edge across the face of the tile. Then cut the tile along the marked line *(box, pages 88-89),* using tile nippers if right-angled notches are needed at the sink's corners.

8 **Buttering a trim tile.** To spread mastic on a tile — to butter it, as the professionals say — scoop about ½ cup of mastic onto the end of a tile trowel; the adhesive manufacturer's instructions will specify whether to use the trowel's V-notched or square-notched end. Rest the end against the wide side of your inside-corner trim tile — usually a piece with a miter cut at one end or a molded right angle that covers both legs of the L. Set the trowel blade at a 45° angle to the tile's back. Slide the blade along the tile, steadily decreasing its angle to squeeze smooth, ¼-inch-thick strips of mastic through the notches onto the tile's back. Apply mastic to the tile's narrow side in the same way. ▶

87

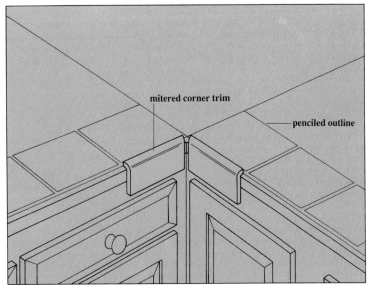

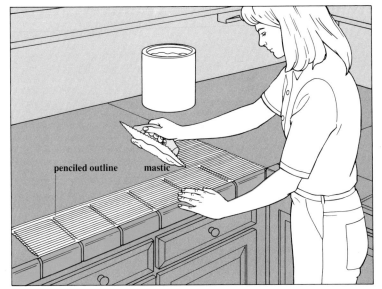

9 **Setting the corner trim.** If your trim pieces for the inside corner are mitered and match the lengths of the counter tiles *(above)*, align the other ends of each mastic-coated piece with the tile line marked in Step 6, and press the trim against the counter's edge. If your mitered inside-corner trim tiles are longer than the counter tiles *(box, opposite)*, position the mitered end of each piece 1/16 inch from the corner, to allow space for a grout joint, before gluing the piece down. If you are using L-shaped trim, center the piece on the corner. After completing the appropriate inside-corner trim, butter and set the trim for any outside corner — usually a single right-angled piece.

10 **Preparing for flat tiles.** Working from the inside corner, butter and set trim tiles on the counter's front edge *(Steps 8-9)*, then set trim tiles on the ends in the same way. Trowel about 1 cup of mastic onto the counter at the corner of the L (or, lacking an L, one end of the counter). Rest whichever trowel edge the mastic manufacturer recommends (V-notched or square-notched) against the counter. Hold the blade at a 45° angle to the surface, and slide it sideways across a 2-foot width of counter, spreading ridges of mastic from the front edge to the backsplash; the penciled layout from Step 6 should be visible between the ridges of mastic. Proceed immediately to Step 11; mastic dries in 10 to 20 minutes.

Three Techniques for Cutting Tile

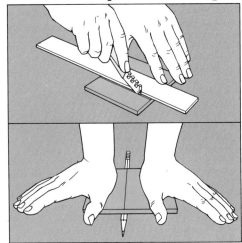

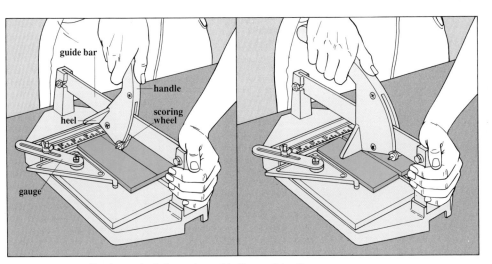

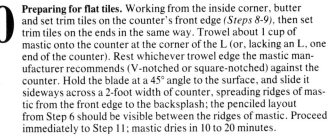

Using a glass cutter. Align a straightedge with the cutting line penciled on the tile. Pull the wheel of a glass cutter smoothly along the straightedge *(above, top)*, pressing down hard. Place the scored line face up over a pencil, and press down on both sides of the tile *(above, bottom)* until it breaks in two.

Using a tile cutter. Set the marked tile on the padded base of the tile cutter, with the cutting line perpendicular to the tile cutter's fence. Lift the heel of the handle, which pushes the scoring wheel down, and pull the handle forward until the wheel touches the tile's far edge. Then place the wheel against the marked line, set the triangular metal gauge against the tile's right side and tighten the gauge's thumbscrew, so you can cut identical tiles without marking them. Pressing down firmly on the front of the handle, keep the handle's heel up while you slide the handle back along its guide bar, scoring the tile *(above, left)*. To snap the tile, lower the handle's heel until its base rests in the middle of the tile and press gently on the handle *(above, right)*.

11   **Tiling the countertop.** At the intersection of the trim-tile lines, press a tile into the mastic with the palm of your hand. Embed the tile with a slight twisting motion, and align its edges with the penciled outline. Working outward toward the backsplash and the counter's opposite end, rapidly embed subsequent tiles in a stair-step pattern, using spacers or a lath joint gauge to maintain even spacing. With a slightly damp sponge, wipe away any mastic that may have squeezed up between tiles. ▶

A Layout Trick for Trim Tile

If your trim tiles are longer than the countertop tiles, lay out the trim after Step 9: Hold two dry trim tiles beside the inside corner, leaving space for joints. Leapfrog tiles to within two tile lengths of the next obstacle — a corner piece or a wall. If further leapfrogging would leave more than half a tile, set the tile *(Step 9)*. Otherwise, measure between the last tile and the obstacle, subtract for three joints and cut two trim pieces (for the counter's ends) to half this length.

Using tile nippers. For corner cuts or curved cuts, such as those required to fit tiles around plumbing pipes, first put on safety goggles. Hold a marked tile face up, and position the jaws of tile nippers ⅛ inch from the edge nearest the cutting line. Squeeze the handles until the nippers' jaws bite off a bit of tile. Continue taking ⅛-inch bites until you reach the cutting line.

Almost every tile countertop requires specially cut tiles for the edges of the sink opening, for the ends and back of the counter, and for the backsplash. A tile dealer will cut tiles (for a small fee) on a water-cooled diamond saw; but in most instances it is more convenient just to measure each piece as the job progresses, and then cut it by one of the methods shown at left.

When only a few straight cuts are needed, an inexpensive glass cutter *(far left)* can score the tiles so that they will snap neatly in two. Layouts that involve many cuts call for two special tools, which can be borrowed from a tile dealer, rented or bought: A tile cutter scores and snaps tile in two quick, foolproof steps *(center left),* and pliers-like tile nippers *(near left)* cut curves and corners by repeatedly biting off bits of tile.

None of these methods is suitable for straight cuts less than 1 inch from a tile's edge (whether to make a wide piece or a narrow one) or for straight cuts on curved trim tile. Tile layouts are designed to obviate such cuts; but when they are unavoidable, have a tile dealer make them. Alternatively, fit a hacksaw with a silicon-carbide blade, hold each tile face up and saw through it — a job that will take about 5 minutes per tile.

Learning to cut tile takes a bit of practice; tile dealers often will give away scrap tile to be used for this purpose. When you begin to cut tiles in earnest, smooth the cut edges with a 6-inch-long medium Carborundum® stone or a similar silicon-carbide whetstone. Rub the stone along the razor-sharp glazed side of each cut edge, repeatedly sliding the stone toward the tile's unglazed side and lifting the stone on the return stroke to prevent chipping.

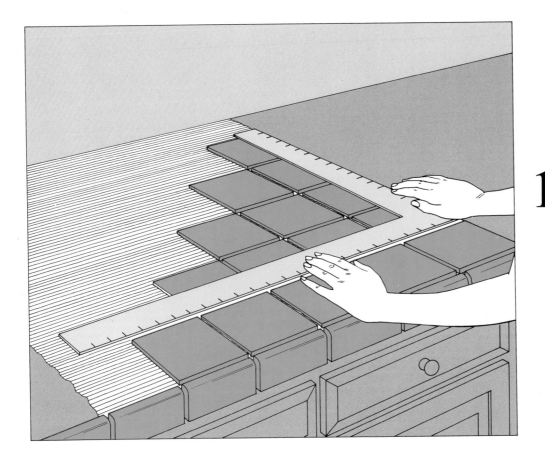

12 **Straightening the tiles.** As you complete each row or column, quickly place one arm of a carpenter's square on the tiles and align the other arm with a perpendicular reference — use the trim-tile line for rows, the counter's edge for columns. Press on any errant tiles with your palm, and slide them inch-meal through the mastic until the row or column is perfectly straight.

Tiling an Old Backsplash

For a tile counter, the ideal backsplash is one or several rows of tile cemented directly onto the wall behind it. However, most old plastic-laminate counters do already have a wooden backsplash, usually ¾ inch thick and about 4 inches high. When tiles are laid on such a counter, the backsplash can sometimes be unscrewed from beneath and pried away so that the wall can be tiled. But often the old backsplash resists removal; in these cases, it can be covered with tile.

The front face of the backsplash is covered with the same type of flat tile used in the countertop. The backsplash top is covered with bullnose tiles, whose rounded edges overlap the square-edged flat tiles; to fit these tiles, hold each piece face down atop the backsplash, with its rounded edge against the wall, and use the technique illustrated in Step 13 to mark and cut the tile. The backsplash's rectangular end is covered with a custom-cut double-bullnose tile, which is rounded on two adjacent edges.

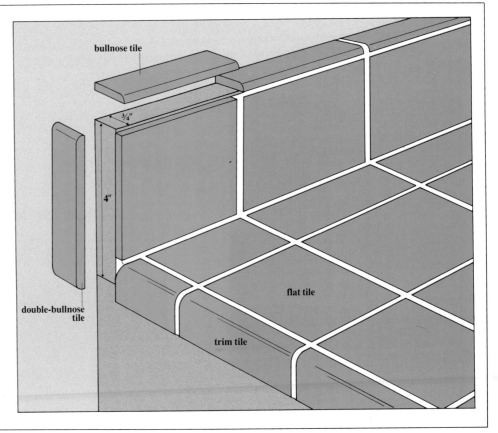

bullnose tile

¾"

4"

double-bullnose tile

flat tile

trim tile

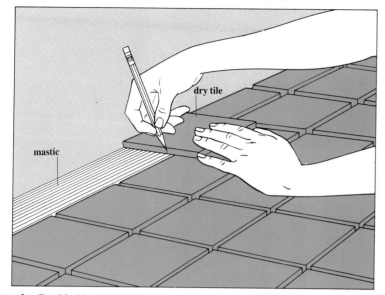

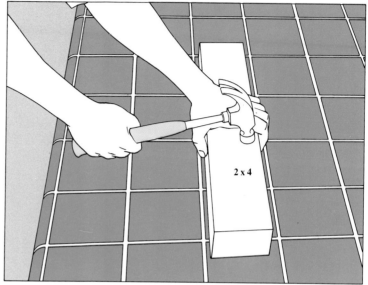

13 **Marking the final tile.** If the last tile in a column must be cut to fit, place a dry tile face down atop the final full tile. Set the dry tile's back edge against the wall or backsplash, and align its sides with the underlying tile. Mark the location of the underlying tile's inner edge on the edges of the upper tile. From these marks, measure toward the backsplash the width of one grout joint and make a second set of marks, then draw a pencil line across the tile's face between the new marks. Cut the tile *(box, pages 88-89)* along this line and embed it in mastic, butting the cut end against the wall.

14 **Leveling the tiles.** Hold a straight 2-by-4 about 18 inches long on the counter's front edge, and tap the board with a hammer until it sits flat on every trim tile. This process is known among professionals as beating in the tile, although actually the blows should be quite gentle. Working toward the wall or backsplash, center the board on each row of tiles and beat them in similarly, then slide the board to the other side of the newly tiled section, and beat in the remaining half of the newly set tiles. Wipe away with a damp sponge any mastic that squeezes up between tiles, then tile the remainder of the counter in 2-foot-wide sections, repeating Steps 10-14.

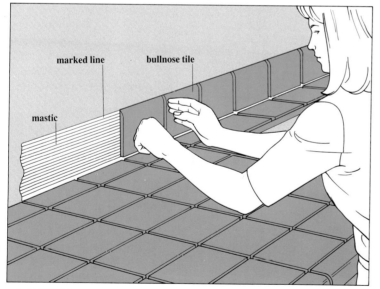

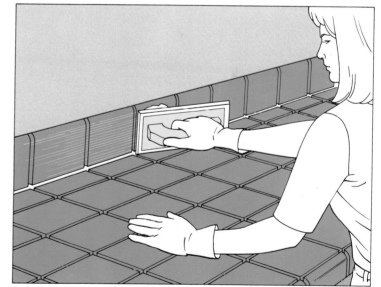

15 **Making a backsplash.** Draw a horizontal line at the planned height of the backsplash, and spread mastic *(Step 10)* to this height from the corner of the L along 2 feet of one wall. Set flat tiles in the mastic *(Step 11)*, leaving a joint space below the first row of tiles and aligning vertical joints with the countertop's column joints; the corner tiles from the adjacent walls will butt snugly together. (They will be sealed later with latex caulk rather than grout.) At the backsplash's top and side edges, use flat bullnose tile; the side pieces should align with the outside edges of the flat countertop tile. Beat in the newly set tiles *(Step 14)*; then tile the rest of the backsplash, always working in 2-foot sections.

16 **Grouting the backsplash.** Let the mastic cure undisturbed for 24 hours. Then, wearing rubber gloves, mix cement-based grout in a paint bucket according to the manufacturer's instructions. Scoop about ½ cup of grout onto the end of a rubber-faced float, and slide the float's end across the backsplash, steadily decreasing the angle from an initial 45° to squeeze grout onto the tile. When the float is empty, hold it at a 45° angle to the wall, set the tip of the float's end between tiles and firmly press grout into each joint. Stir the grout periodically to keep the pigment from settling unevenly. ▶

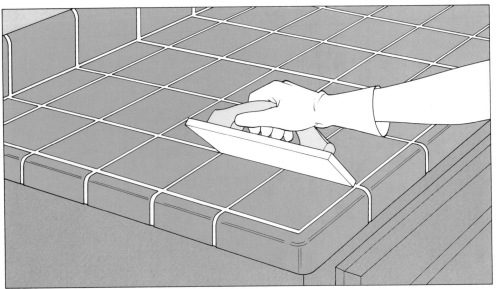

17 **Grouting the countertop.** Using the rubber-faced float, scoop about 1 cup of grout onto one end of the counter. Then rest the float's long edge on the counter, set its face at a 45° angle to the countertop, and sweep the float diagonally across a 2-foot width of countertop, steadily decreasing the angle. When all joints in the section are filled with grout, hold the float at a 45° angle, set it lengthwise on each joint and use its edge to push grout into the joint (above). Grout the rest of the countertop in similar 2-foot-wide sections, then grout the trim tile as in Step 16.

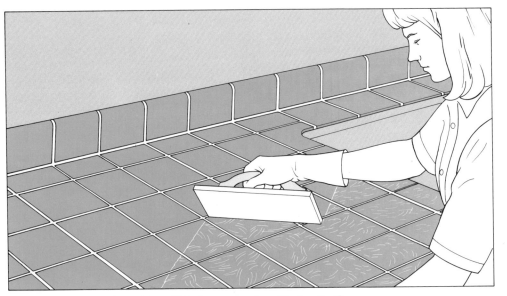

18 **Finishing the grout joints.** Slide the narrow edge of the handle of an old toothbrush along each joint; if this packs the grout below the tile face, immediately regrout the joint (Steps 16-17) flush with the tile. Clean the rubber-faced float, hold its face at a 60° angle to the tile and use it as a squeegee, sliding the edge diagonally across all newly tiled surfaces to remove excess grout. Wipe the tile with a damp sponge and let it dry for about half an hour; when a haze forms, polish the tile with a soft, dry cloth. Tape kraft paper over the counter and backsplash, and let the grout cure for three days, then spray all surfaces with an aerosol can of silicone sealant.

The Art of Painting Tile

Hand-painted glazed tiles such as those at right will add intriguing accents to a ceramic counter or backsplash, weaving one of a room's visual themes — a wallpaper design, perhaps, or a period ornament — into the simple geometry of plain tiles. When decorated and fired, the tiles can be laid in rows to border a backsplash or counter, or interspersed at intervals among unpainted ones.

For painting tile, you have a choice of two distinctly different ceramic overglazes. Ceramic decorating color such as Versacolor™ paint is sold by dealers of school art supplies; it comes only in sets of eight tubes of bright colors, and creates the bold, opaque finish on the tile at near right. China paint, which is sold by ceramics-supply dealers, generally comes in two parts — a tinted powder and a conditioning oil — that are mixed before use. Available in a great range of colors, china paint produces delicate figures that resemble watercolor paintings (far right). Both china paint and Versacolor paint must be thinned with turpentine before use.

A ceramics-supply dealer will fire your painted tiles for a small fee. Whichever type of overglaze you select, ask for a kiln setting of Cone 018 — a designation that specifies both firing temperature and time.

An overglaze's final color always is somewhat problematic: Both types tend to darken during firing. And when the basic Versacolor glazes are mixed to obtain intermediate hues, the results cannot be predicted; reds and oranges are particularly capricious. To overcome these problems, paint test tiles before embarking on full-scale production. Mix a tiny quantity of each hue, and fire a painted tile for a first color approximation, then mix sufficient paint for all of your tiles, fire another test tile and seal each mixture in an airtight jar.

When the color of the fired test tiles is right, paint all of your tiles with the same mixtures. Let the tiles dry overnight, then use a razor-blade knife to repair ragged edges and to scrape away any smudges. Do not stack the painted tiles; instead, carry them to the kiln side-by-side in flat boxes.

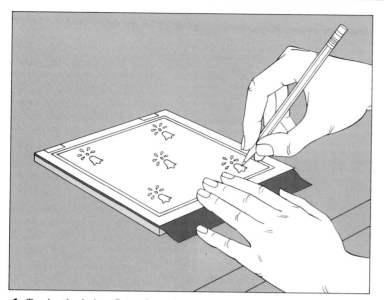

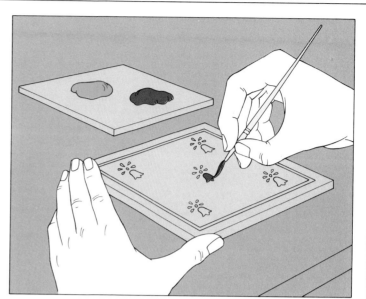

1 **Tracing the design.** Cut a piece of tracing paper or lightweight bond paper to the tile's surface dimensions, and draw or trace the design on the paper. Clean each tile in turn with alcohol, then tape the design to adjacent corners of the tile. Slip carbon paper beneath the design and trace it with a pencil, pressing down firmly to make distinct carbon lines on the tile; the lines will burn off in the kiln.

2 **Painting the tiles.** Using the carbon lines to guide your brush strokes, paint figures in the center of a tile, then the outer figures: With china paint, first outline a figure with a soft, fine brush, then brush on the lightest interior color, followed by successively darker ones. With ceramic decorating color, load the brush heavily and lay the paint on thickly, so that the opaque overglaze completely obscures the underlying tile.

Design painted with Versacolor paint

Design painted with china paint

Plastic laminate: Handsome and durable

Despite the visual rewards to be had by the installation of a new laminate countertop *(below)*, some people are daunted by the prospect of working with the large sheets of plastic-coated material and the fast-acting contact cement that holds it. In fact, with the right tools and a little know-how, resurfacing a counter with laminate can be a fairly simple task.

Plastic-laminate sheets — 1/16 inch in thickness — range from 2 to 5 feet in width and 6 to 12 feet in length. But most dealers stock only 4-by-8-foot sheets, and in a limited selection of styles. If you place an order for a special finish and color, you can ask for sheets that will approximate the size of your counter. (Keep in mind that you will need to cover the backsplash and the counter edges as well as the top.) Store the laminate in your kitchen for 48 hours before installing it, to give it time to adjust to room temperature and humidity.

Although the material is stiff and brittle, plastic laminate is sturdy enough for shaping with woodworking tools. New laminate can be applied over old, as demonstrated here. If the counter ends are accessible, you can leave the counter in place; otherwise, use the technique on page 71, Step 2 to remove the counter before covering it — and follow Step 13, page 74 to replace it afterward.

To trim the laminate, you will need a router — a power tool *(page 99)* that is available from rental shops. You will have to buy two carbide-tipped router bits: one for flush cuts, one for bevels.

Other tools for the task are fairly basic: a saber saw with a fine-toothed blade (at least 20 teeth to the inch), an orbital sander, hand roller, file, sanding block and, if you have to cut openings, a drill. You need nonflammable contact cement, plus a ¾-inch natural-bristled paintbrush, a roller tray and a mohair-covered paint roller to spread it.

Before you start, have an expert remove the sink or any appliance that is set into your counter. Make sure that the counter surface is even and that existing laminate is glued firmly. Repair any gouges or loose edges *(page 101)*. If the counter is rimmed with metal bands, remove them; fill any holes in the edges with wood putty. With an orbital sander, thoroughly sand all the surfaces to be covered — both to eliminate bumps and to roughen old laminate so it will bond to the adhesive. Use a vacuum cleaner or paintbrush to remove all sanding dust.

As you plan your cuts, reserve the factory-cut laminate edges for counter edges that cannot be smoothed out with the router — the edges where the counter abuts the backsplash, for example.

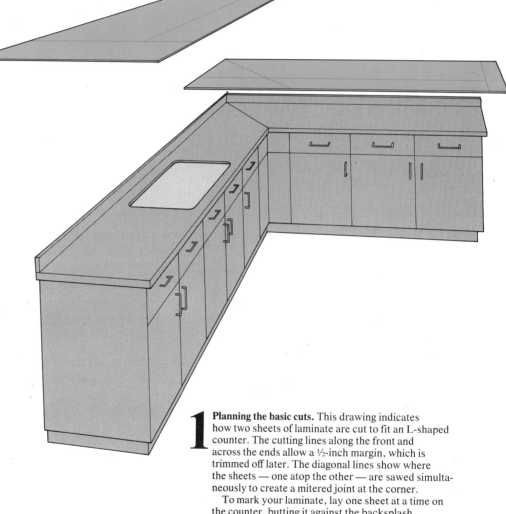

1 **Planning the basic cuts.** This drawing indicates how two sheets of laminate are cut to fit an L-shaped counter. The cutting lines along the front and across the ends allow a ½-inch margin, which is trimmed off later. The diagonal lines show where the sheets — one atop the other — are sawed simultaneously to create a mitered joint at the corner.

To mark your laminate, lay one sheet at a time on the counter, butting it against the backsplash. While a helper holds the sheet, draw lines on its underside at the counter edges. Turn the sheet face down on a flat surface, and draw cutting lines ½ inch outside these lines. Do not draw lines for the diagonal cut at this stage. If there is not room to get the sheets onto the counter, measure the counter's length and width, add a ½-inch margin, and draw the front and end cutting lines. With the sheets upside down, draw lines like a mirror image of the counter; keep factory edges to butt against the backsplash. ►

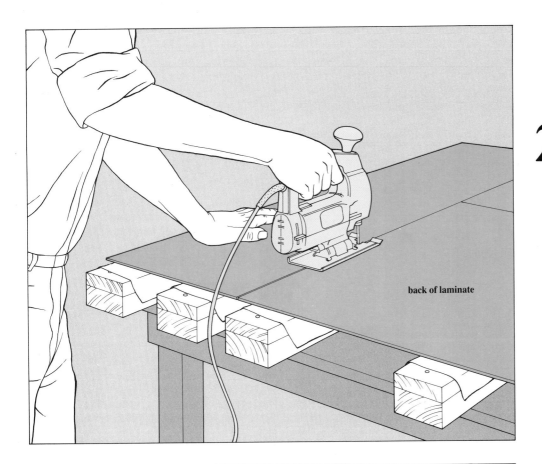

2 **Cutting the laminate.** Lay a sheet of laminate face down on the work surface, using several boards at least 3 feet long to support the sheet on each side of the cutting line; cover them with brown wrapping paper to protect the face of the laminate. The supports should be about 2½ inches high to prevent the tip of the saber saw's blade from striking the work surface. Here, 1-by-4s are nailed to 2-by-4s to form the supports.

Wearing safety goggles, steady the sheet with one hand as you start the saber saw and make the cut. Rearrange the supports, and cut on the lengthwise line; stop the saw and move the supports as necessary.

Reserving factory-cut edges for the backsplash, cut strips for the counter edges from the remaining laminate. On each strip, allow ½-inch margins all around.

back of laminate

4 **Applying adhesive for an edge strip.** Use a vacuum cleaner or paintbrush to thoroughly dust the back of a laminate strip and the counter edge to which you will bond it. Spread contact cement onto the counter edge *(above),* using a ¾-inch natural-bristled brush and making certain that you cover the entire surface. Then brush the adhesive onto the strip of laminate. Allow the adhesive to dry for approximately 15 minutes; it is ready for bonding when a clean piece of brown wrapping paper will not stick to it.

3 **Cutting the mitered corner.** Place the two panels face up on the counter, butting their overlapping ends into the corner. Mark the underside of the bottom panel at the front edge of the counter's L-shaped corner. Now place the panels face down on wood supports, realigning them as if you had inverted the assemblage as a unit. Join them with C clamps, protecting their faces from clamp marks with paper and scraps of wood. Draw a straight line from the outside corner of the L through the mark you made at the inside angle. Measure from an edge of the saber saw's base plate to the edge of the blade, and clamp a wood strip at that distance from, and parallel to, the diagonal cutting line. Using the wood strip as a guide, cut through both sheets of laminate at once to ensure a snug joint across the corner of the counter.

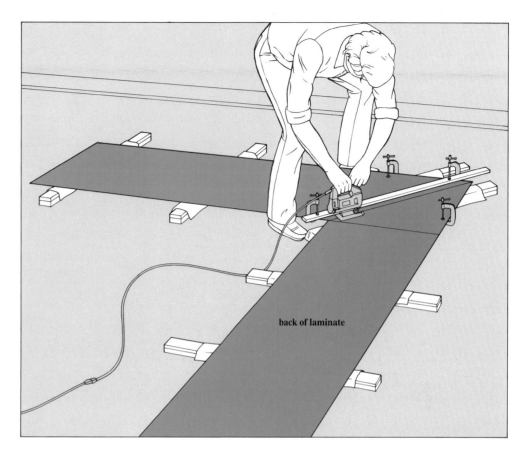

back of laminate

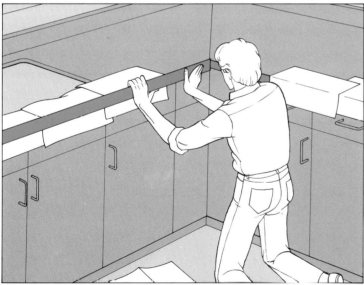

5 **Positioning an edge strip.** Drape pieces of brown wrapping paper over the edge of the counter so that the two adhesive-covered surfaces cannot make contact until you are ready. Holding the laminate with both hands — and with a helper holding the other end, if necessary — position the strip close to the counter edge, with the ½-inch margin extending evenly above, below and at the end. If an end of the strip is to meet an inside corner, as here, butt it into that corner now. Starting at one end — here, in the corner — pull out the first piece of paper, and press the strip onto the counter edge. Work your way along the length of the strip, pulling out the brown paper and pressing the laminate into position.

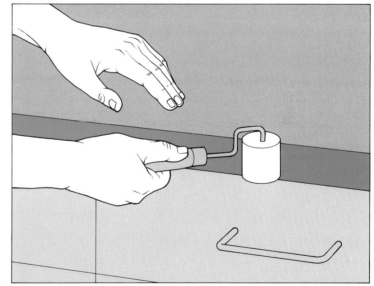

6 **Rolling the laminate for a strong bond.** Immediately after attaching the strip to the counter edge, roll the face of the laminate with a hand roller or a rolling pin, applying firm, even pressure. Roll the entire length of the strip several times to ensure good adhesion.

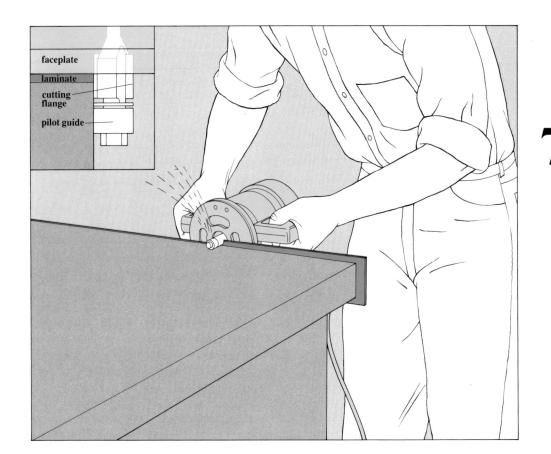

faceplate
laminate
cutting flange
pilot guide

7 **Trimming the laminate.** Fit a router (*opposite, bottom*) with a carbide-tipped flush-cutting bit. Protect yourself with safety goggles and a dust mask. Hold the router in a horizontal position, with the lower part of its faceplate flat against the newly laminated edge, the bit just above the rim of excess laminate.

Switch the motor on and slowly lower the router so the bit cuts into the laminate. When the pilot guide hits the counter, move the router from right to left, trimming the strip flush with the countertop.

Use the router to trim the protruding margins of the strip on all sides, moving the machine counterclockwise around the counter edge. Then clean, laminate and trim the other counter edges.

10 **Covering the counter.** Lay wood strips across the counter at 1-foot intervals, then put the laminate, adhesive side down, on the wood strips. The strips will keep the laminate from sticking to the counter before you are ready. Butt the panel's factory-cut edge against the backsplash, and set the tip of the diagonally cut end in the corner. Pull out the wood strip nearest to the corner while pressing that part of the laminate down with a sweeping motion, so no air is trapped beneath the panel. Work along the counter, pulling out the wood strips one by one. Immediately roll the surface several times with the hand roller, applying extra pressure near the edges.

Install the second panel, making sure first to form a tight diagonal seam at the corner. Roll the seam thoroughly. ▶

8 **Sanding the edges of the strips.** After laminating all of the counter edges and trimming the strips with a router, smooth the top edges of the trimmed laminate *(above)* with a sanding block and medium (80-grit) sandpaper. Then again clean off all dust.

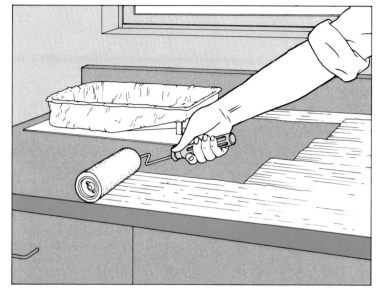

9 **Spreading adhesive for the countertop.** Take a panel of the laminate you have cut for the countertop, and lay it face down on newspapers spread on the kitchen floor. Pour a layer of contact cement into the well of a paint tray lined with aluminum foil. Roll a mohair-covered paint roller in the contact cement, then on the back of the laminate, making sure the adhesive covers the entire surface; apply a slightly thicker coat near the edges of the panel. Then roll adhesive onto the countertop surface and allow it to dry until a piece of brown wrapping paper will not stick to it — approximately 15 minutes.

Using a Router Safely

A router is a high-speed power tool for cutting and shaping wood and plastic. To form flush and bevel cuts in laminate, fit the router with carbide-tipped bits and adjust their cutting depth as shown below. Because a bit creates so much dust and throws it so far, put on safety goggles and a dust mask before using the router. Always hold its handles firmly; always unplug it when it is not in use. If you rent a router, get instructions for handling it; different models can vary widely.

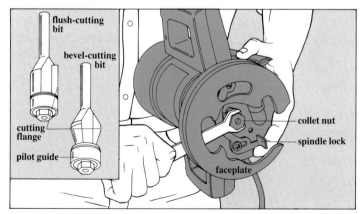

1 **Installing a bit.** Be certain the router is unplugged. Then, for this model, reach underneath the faceplate and pull the tab of the spindle lock with your fingers; the spindle lock will engage the spindle and hold it in place. Loosen the collet nut by turning it counterclockwise with a collet wrench. For trimming plastic laminate, insert a flush-cutting or bevel-cutting bit *(inset)* into the collet as far as it will go. Pull the bit outward a fraction of an inch and tighten the collet nut.

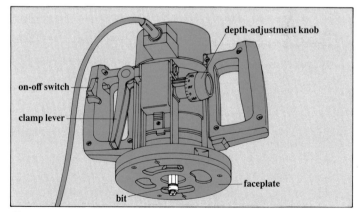

2 **Adjusting the cutting depth.** With the router unplugged, swing the clamp lever on this model to the unlocked position. Then turn the depth-adjustment knob, which raises and lowers the motor and bit in relation to the faceplate, and relock the clamp lever. For use on laminate, the cutting edges of a bit need extend only a fraction of an inch beyond the faceplate. Take special care in adjusting the cutting depth of a bevel bit. The farther its cutting edges extend beyond the faceplate, the deeper the bevel it will cut. When making a bevel cut *(page 101, Step 13)*, try a shallow setting first to make sure you will not be cutting through the laminate to the wood counter beneath.

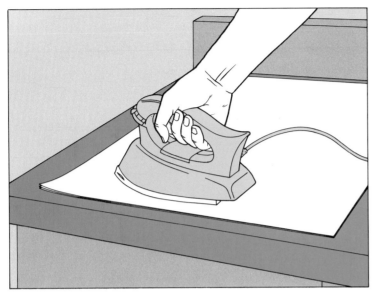

11 **Ironing out a bubble.** If the contact cement fails to form a bond at some spot, the new laminate surface probably will rise there in a low bump, or bubble. Place brown paper over the bubble and put a hot iron (set for ironing cotton) on the paper. Let the iron stand until the laminate feels hot to the touch; the heat will soften the adhesive so it regains its stickiness. Remove the iron and paper, and roll the hand roller or rolling pin over the area with steady pressure until the surface is cool again and smooth.

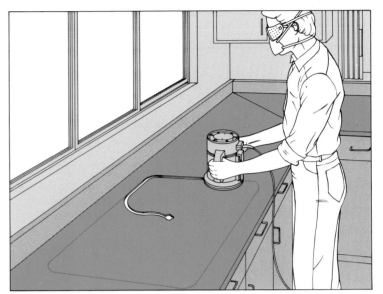

12 **Cutting the sink opening.** Drill several overlapping holes in the center of the laminate over the sink opening, until you have formed a hole large enough to admit the flush-cutting router bit. Put on your dust mask and safety goggles. Start the router; lower the flush-cutting bit into the hole and move the router toward the back of the sink opening, cutting a channel as you go. When the pilot guide on the bit hits the back edge of the sink opening, move the router clockwise. The pilot guide will help you to keep the bit at the edge as you work your way around the entire opening.

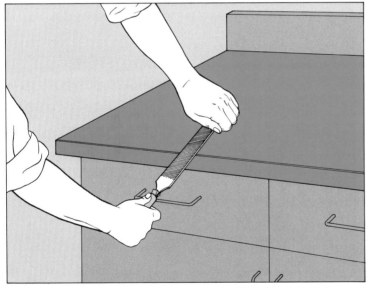

14 **Smoothing the bevels.** Finish the bevels with a 14-inch single-cut mill file, applying pressure on the forward stroke. Run a finger-tip along each angle to make certain that no rough spots remain; they might later result in cracks or scuff marks. Be especially careful at the inside corners, which are particularly prone to cracking if they are not filed smooth.

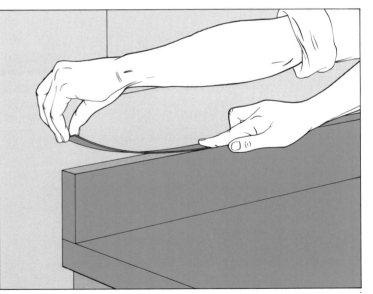

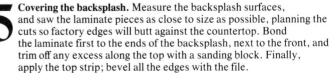

15 **Covering the backsplash.** Measure the backsplash surfaces, and saw the laminate pieces as close to size as possible, planning the cuts so factory edges will butt against the countertop. Bond the laminate first to the ends of the backsplash, next to the front, and trim off any excess along the top with a sanding block. Finally, apply the top strip; bevel all the edges with the file.

13 **Trimming the countertop.** Put masking tape on the newly laminated counter edges so the router bit's pilot guide will not damage them as you trim the margins from the countertop panels. Hold the router — still fitted with the flush-cutting bit — vertical, its faceplate partly resting on the countertop. Start the motor, and slowly cut into the laminate overhang until the pilot guide reaches the counter edge. Move the router left to right all along the counter. Next fit the router with a 22° bevel bit and, again moving left to right, bevel the seam at the top of the counter edge *(right and inset)*. The beveled joint will resist chipping and give the counter a finished appearance. Wherever two pieces of laminate meet at a 90° angle, bevel the seam.

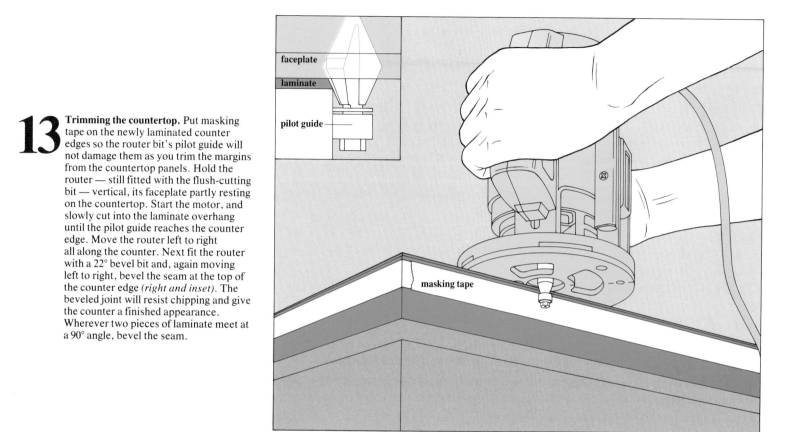

Special Treatment for Damaged Counters

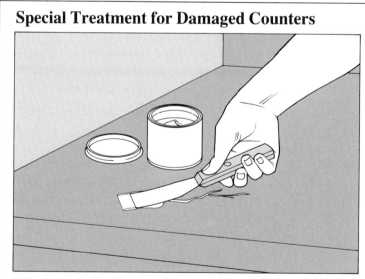

Filling the cracks. To prepare an old laminated counter for resurfacing, fill minor cracks and gouges with wood putty. Push the putty into the crack with a flexible-bladed putty knife; pressing down to bend the blade slightly, pull the knife across the area first from one angle and then from another, until the entire hole is packed and slightly overfilled. Let the putty dry overnight, then sand it flush with the countertop. If the old laminate is marred by large cracks, the counter will have to be replaced.

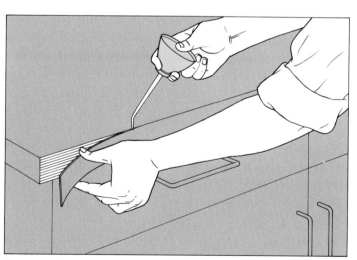

Removing loose laminate. If a section of the laminate edge is loose, remove it before re-covering the counter. First heat the adhesive, either with an iron *(opposite)* or with a hair dryer. If the adhesive softens, pull the laminate off slowly as you continue heating it. Should heat not do the job, use an oilcan to squirt nonflammable adhesive solvent under the laminate *(above)* as you slowly pull the piece away. Then sand the counter edge, and glue on another strip of laminate — to run the full length of the edge or to serve as a gap-filling foundation for new laminate if it is only part of one edge. If the laminate top is partially loose — or if water seepage has damaged the wood counter — replace the whole counter.

Paint and wallpaper

The walls and ceiling that form the backdrop for a kitchen should be as practical as any other element of the room — and as handsome. Depending on your taste and budget, these areas can be covered with anything from polyurethane-coated plank paneling to glazed tiles — even, in the case of the ceiling, with old-fashioned embossed and enameled tin. However, for stylish transformations that are easy to effect and economical besides, the stand-bys are paint and wallpaper for covering walls; for ceilings, paint excels.

The two sorts of paint suited to kitchen walls and ceilings are those best suited to cabinets: latex and alkyd *(page 22)*. And the same compromises apply when you are making a choice between them. Latex dries faster; alkyd is hardier. In either material, a mat, or low-glare, paint cannot be scrubbed often or well. But glossy finishes have the drawback of reflecting a lot of light and thus revealing every patch, bulge or imperfection in the wall or ceiling they cover. You may decide to sacrifice cleanability in order to minimize surface imperfections.

The most long-lasting wallpapers for kitchens are not plain paper nor, in many cases, any kind of paper at all. Vinyl-coated papers have a minuscule layer of plastic that serves only to make them washable, not scrubbable. By contrast, the film layer on paper-backed vinyls or fabric-backed vinyls provides substantial reinforcement. These wallpapers, together with the solid vinyls, are scrubbable and grease- and stain-resistant — all properties of special value in kitchen use.

In the matter of color, a pale hue is the usual prescription for giving kitchens a sense of spaciousness. Rich colors, on the other hand, can help bring overlarge rooms down to size. Sunlit kitchens can be cooled with blues, purples and greens, while dark kitchens are brightened by shades of yellow, beige and white.

Wallpapers offer the extra option of patterns. For a kitchen, where appliances and cabinets divide many of the wall spaces into rectangles of various sizes, the most adaptable patterns are vertical stripes and small-scale designs. When you select a pattern, always check the sample book to find the length of each repeat — the distance from where a complete design starts to where it begins to repeat. The longer the repeat, the more paper you will waste when you start matching one strip to another.

Pattern matching, in fact, becomes a basic consideration in buying and later in hanging the material. A vertical stripe or a so-called random-match pattern will pose no problems. A straight-match pattern needs to be aligned so the design will repeat horizontally from strip to strip. In a drop-match pattern, the design repeats diagonally, and the alignment point of one side of a strip lies halfway between two alignment points on the opposite side; the most economical way to match this kind of pattern is to cut alternate strips from two rolls of paper.

You can determine how much wallpaper or paint you need by some simple calculations of area. For a rectangular ceiling, measure its length and width, then multiply these figures to find its square footage. For an L-shaped ceiling and for all walls, measure and multiply each rectangular section separately, then add them together. To calculate how much paint you will need for the room's trim, allow about 21 square feet for each side of a door and 15 square feet for a window. For a baseboard, multiply its height by its total length.

To paint over a smooth surface, estimate one gallon per coat for each 400 square feet. For rough or previously unpainted surfaces, figure 350 square feet to a gallon.

For paperhanging, you need to determine how many rolls of wallpaper you must have. Although wallpaper widths range from 15 to 54 inches, each standard single roll holds 36 square feet of material. After trimming and matching, the roll should cover about 30 square feet. For your kitchen, divide the total square footage you want to cover by 30. If this computation produces a fractional remainder, round the answer upward to the next whole number so you will not run out of wallpaper midway through the project.

Applying new color with brush and roller

When painting your kitchen, work from top to bottom: Tackle the ceiling first, then paint each wall in turn. For each surface, start by outlining the area with brushwork and finish by filling in the remaining space with a roller.

Roller work goes fastest when done with overlapping, nearly parallel strokes. Outlining, by contrast, calls for two different techniques. The first, called cutting in, uses back-and-forth strokes along the edges of the ceiling or on walls where matching paints will meet. The other technique is beading: A thin paint line, called a bead, is drawn along an edge of a surface where one paint meets another or where paint abuts another material: wallpaper or window glass, for example.

After the ceiling and walls comes the trim: baseboards and the frames of windows and doors. Here, all work is best done with brushes: natural-bristled for alkyd paint, nylon-bristled for latex. Ideally, you should have a pair of 2- or 2½-inch trim brushes — one with chisel-edged bristles, one with bristles cut crosswise at an angle — and a 3½- or 4-inch wall brush.

The most convenient roller has a 7-inch head covered with a ¼-inch nap for applying glossy paint, a ½-inch nap for mat paint. The roller's handle should be threaded inside to hold an extension pole, which you will want for painting the ceiling and high areas on the walls. A stepladder is a must for outlining edges at the ceiling. To hold the paint, you need both a pail and a roller pan with a grate.

Preliminary to painting, clear the walls of all movable objects, undress the windows and empty the counters. If surfaces are painted and in good condition, simply wash them with a solution of one part ammonia to six parts water or with a heavy-duty household detergent. Chipped or blistered paint should be evened, and glossy paint roughened slightly, with steel wool or sandpaper. Fill cracks or small gouges in plaster or wallboard with spackling compound *(page 104);* repair woodwork with putty *(page 23, Step 4).* If you intend to put latex paint over alkyd, apply a latex primer first. If you will be painting alkyd over latex, seal the latex first with an alkyd primer.

If the walls are papered with vinyl or other strippable covering, peel it away — starting from the top corner of each strip. Removing other coverings will require more effort. Cut horizontal slits in the wallpaper at intervals of 8 to 10 inches, then wet the paper with a solution of detergent and warm water or with a liquid paper remover. Wait 10 minutes or so, then scrape off the softened paper with a flexible-bladed taping or putty knife.

If the soaking process fails, you can rent an electric steamer to loosen the wallpaper. After stripping the paper from the walls, wash them with a heavy-duty detergent to remove traces of paper and adhesive; let the walls dry thoroughly.

Just before you start painting, turn off the electric power at the circuit breaker or fuse box. Then unscrew the switch and receptacle plates from the walls. Loosen the screws of the mounting plate that holds any ceiling or wall fixture, so you can pull the plate away in order to paint behind it; tape a plastic bag over the fixture. Finally spread dropcloths, preferably plastic, over floors and counters; protect edges with masking tape.

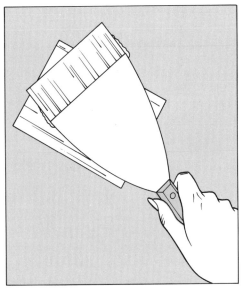

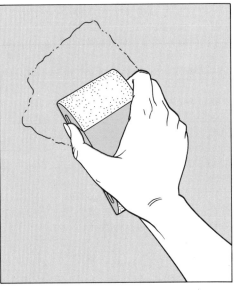

1 **Applying spackling compound.** With a flexible-bladed putty knife or — as shown — a taping knife, press a thin layer of ready-mixed vinyl spackling compound into any crack or dent in the kitchen wall or ceiling. Smooth the surface, letting the compound extend in a thin layer about 1 inch beyond the patch. Allow the compound to dry overnight. If a hole is very broad or deep, you may need to refill it when the compound dries and thus shrinks.

2 **Sanding a patch.** Wrap a sanding block with a sheet of fine (150-grit) sandpaper. Using a circular motion, gently sand outward from the center of the dried patch — feathering, or blending, its edges into the surrounding surface. Tap the sanding block occasionally to remove accumulated dust; replace the sandpaper as necessary. Wipe the sanded area gently with a cloth.

3 **Loading a paintbrush.** Pour a layer of paint several inches deep into a pail; cover the paint can, and set it aside. Dip a natural-bristled brush, in this case a trim brush 2½ inches wide, partway into the paint so that only the bottom third of the bristles is covered. Tap one flat side of the bristles gently against the dry inner surface of the pail to remove excess paint; flip the brush over, and tap the bristles again.

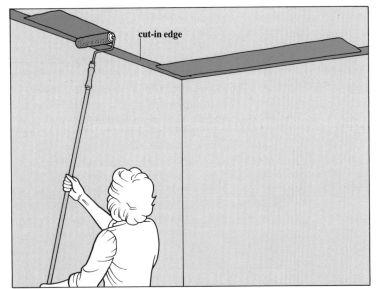

cut-in edge

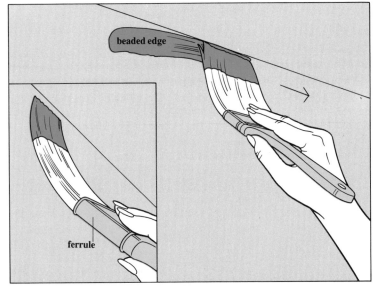

beaded edge

ferrule

6 **Painting a ceiling.** Position the loaded roller so that it will paint along the ceiling's shorter dimension. Keeping the roller as close to the ceiling edge as possible and beginning about 3 feet from the corner, push the roller toward the corner. Next, place the roller 3 feet from the corner along the ceiling's longer dimension, and push the roller toward the corner (above). Make overlapping, almost parallel strokes until you have painted a 3-foot square. To ensure complete coverage and minimize roller marks, go back to your first position and make more back-and-forth strokes perpendicular to and overlapping the first set. Reloading the roller each time, paint successive squares across the ceiling's width, then go back and across again until the ceiling is completely painted.

7 **Beading.** To achieve a precise line of demarcation along an edge where two colors of paint will meet — in this case, where a wall meets the ceiling — use a trim brush with a firmly chiseled bristle edge. Grasp the brush by placing all four fingers on top of its metal ferrule and letting your thumb rest underneath it. Load the brush, and press the bristles flat about ¹⁄₁₆ inch from the edge; a thin line of paint — the bead — will rise to the bristle tips. Without removing the tips from the wall, gently raise the brush until it makes a 45° angle with the wall, then slowly drag the brush along the edge as far as you can comfortably reach. Go back and, holding the brush as before, use the paint already on the wall to draw a line even closer to the ceiling. Repeat along the ceiling edge.

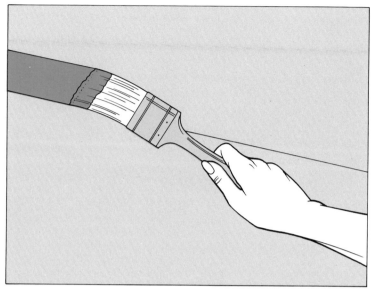

4 **Cutting in.** Start in one corner of the ceiling. Using a trim brush, make long, overlapping strokes from left to right along the ceiling line, keeping the brush parallel to the edge as you work. Repeat these strokes around the entire perimeter of the ceiling.

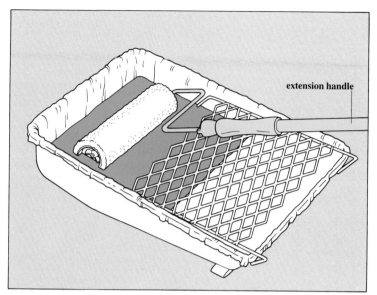

extension handle

5 **Loading a roller.** Line a roller pan with aluminum foil, or wrap the pan in a plastic bag. Fill the well of the pan half full with paint; set the paint can aside. Insert a wire grating over the sloping segment of the pan. For painting the ceiling or the top of a wall, screw a 4-foot extension handle into the threaded base of the roller's handle. Dip the roller into the well of the pan, then roll it up and down the grating two or three times. Dip the roller into the paint once again, and roll it back and forth until the cover is saturated evenly but does not drip.

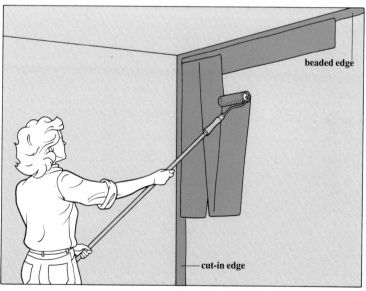

beaded edge

cut-in edge

8 **Painting a large wall area.** After beading along the ceiling edge, cut in along the wall's side edges, along the baseboard, and around such obstacles as doors and windows. Beginning in the top left-hand corner, position a loaded roller parallel to and as close to the ceiling edge as possible and about 3 feet from the corner; then push the roller horizontally toward the corner. Next, place the roller 3 feet below the corner near the left edge of the wall; this time, push the roller toward the ceiling. Immediately, make overlapping, almost parallel, vertical strokes until you have completed a 3-foot square. Reload the roller and make a second square under the first; repeat until you have completed a 3-foot-wide panel from ceiling to baseboard. Continue in this way across the wall.

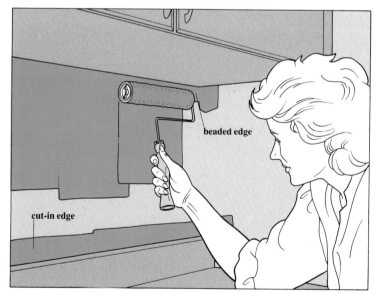

beaded edge

cut-in edge

9 **Painting a small wall area.** Bead or cut in the edges of the area. Load a roller and, starting at one corner, roll paint onto the wall in small rectangular sections. Hold the roller either vertically or horizontally, whichever is more comfortable; most people find vertical strokes less tiring. ▶

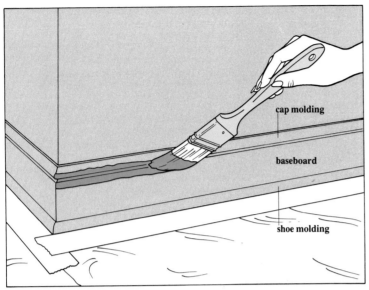

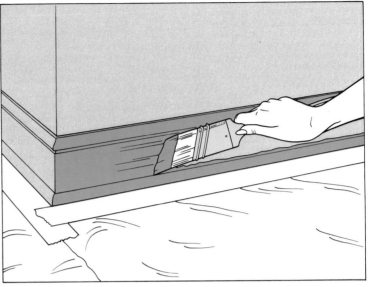

10 **Edging the cap molding.** With an angular trim brush, paint along the crevice between the cap molding and the baseboard for 3 feet. Then load the brush as described in Step 3; but wipe the bristles across the pail rim, and tap the ferrule against the opposite, clean rim to remove more paint. Holding the brush like a pencil, rest the bristles on the cap molding at the top of the baseboard. Exert slight pressure on the tip of the brush to raise a bead of paint, and slowly pull the brush along the top of the baseboard for about 3 feet. As the paint forms a beaded edge, it will coat the cap molding. While the paint is wet, paint the next section of cap molding.

11 **Painting the baseboard.** With the trim brush, paint the quarter-round, or shoe, molding at the bottom of the baseboard; use the same edging-and-beading technique, but point the bristles downward to lay the bead at the floor line. Then, holding the brush parallel to the length of the baseboard, as shown, paint along its vertical face with long, smooth strokes.

The Sequence for a Sash Window

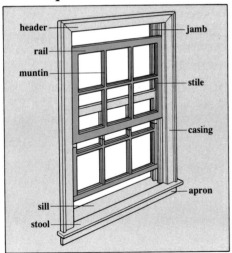

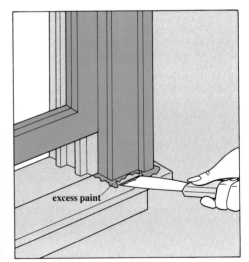

1 **The sashes.** Unscrew all of the hardware. Lift the inside sash almost to the top, then pull down the outside sash. Beading the edges to keep the panes clean, paint the inner strips, or muntins, of the inside sash with a chisel-edged trim brush. Next, paint the outer strips — the horizontal rails, then the vertical stiles. Finally, following the same sequence, paint the exposed strips of the outside sash. Do not paint the bottom edge of either sash.

2 **Completing the frame.** Pushing against their unpainted edges, reverse the positions of the sashes. Paint the remaining sections of the inner and outer strips of the outside sash; paint its top edge. Now paint the top edge of the inside sash. Working downward, paint the underside of the header above the sashes, then the casing that frames the top and sides of the window. Let the paint dry for at least eight hours.

3 **The jambs.** When the paint is dry to the touch, move the sashes up and down to be sure they will not stick. Then push them down, and use a putty knife to lift any blobs of excess paint from the stool. Paint each wood strip of the upper jambs in turn — starting at the back of the frame. Paint the front strip from top to bottom; do not paint metal jamb parts. When the paint dries, raise the sashes. Paint the lower jambs, the stool and apron. Replace the hardware.

The Sequence for a Door

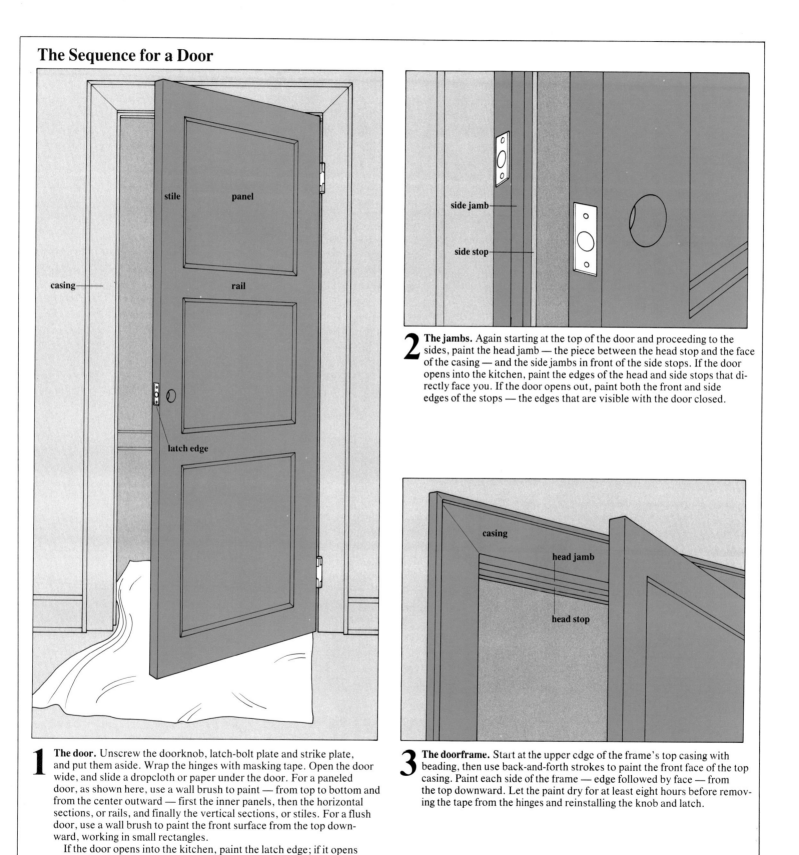

2 **The jambs.** Again starting at the top of the door and proceeding to the sides, paint the head jamb — the piece between the head stop and the face of the casing — and the side jambs in front of the side stops. If the door opens into the kitchen, paint the edges of the head and side stops that directly face you. If the door opens out, paint both the front and side edges of the stops — the edges that are visible with the door closed.

1 **The door.** Unscrew the doorknob, latch-bolt plate and strike plate, and put them aside. Wrap the hinges with masking tape. Open the door wide, and slide a dropcloth or paper under the door. For a paneled door, as shown here, use a wall brush to paint — from top to bottom and from the center outward — first the inner panels, then the horizontal sections, or rails, and finally the vertical sections, or stiles. For a flush door, use a wall brush to paint the front surface from the top downward, working in small rectangles.

If the door opens into the kitchen, paint the latch edge; if it opens outward, paint the hinge edge. Do not paint the top edge.

3 **The doorframe.** Start at the upper edge of the frame's top casing with beading, then use back-and-forth strokes to paint the front face of the top casing. Paint each side of the frame — edge followed by face — from the top downward. Let the paint dry for at least eight hours before removing the tape from the hinges and reinstalling the knob and latch.

Hanging a vinyl-protected pattern

The lively colors and patterns of vinyl wallpapers, such as the one shown below, are protected from wear, tear and kitchen grime by a plastic film. Because the film is flexible, vinyls are unlikely to rip or pull apart as plain wallpapers sometimes do and thus are relatively simple to hang — even for a novice without a helper.

The initial steps in wallpapering, as in painting, are to clear the walls and counters, strip off old paper, wash old paint, and patch cracks or dents *(page 104, Steps 1 and 2)*. If you plan to paint the ceiling or woodwork, do that first.

To create a surface onto which the wallpaper will glide easily, brush or roll oil-based or acrylic primer-sealer over the walls and allow it to dry overnight. The sealer will prevent the wall from absorbing moisture from the paste and thus it will ensure that the wallpaper sticks well and the seams stay shut. The sealer will also make it easier to strip the material when you eventually tire of it.

Turn off the power to the room; unscrew the plates from switches and outlets that will be in your path as you work.

For a place to begin paperhanging, choose an inconspicuous corner: Unless the kitchen's perimeter happens to be a multiple of your wallpaper's width, you will have a mismatch where the last strip

you hang meets the first one. Inside a corner, this mismatch will pass unnoticed.

Because true square corners and vertical walls are unlikely, you will need a chalk line and a plumb bob to establish a vertical starting point. Determining where to start the wallpaper's pattern at the ceiling requires an on-the-spot check *(Step 2)*. After you have done this, you are ready to measure the wall height and add 2-inch margins at the top and bottom to find how long to cut the first strip.

Pasting comes next, and this task varies with the paper chosen. With wallpaper that is not prepasted, adhesive can be applied to the back of the material and the strip smoothed onto the wall. Alternatively, so-called paste-the-wall adhesive can be applied to the wall itself and the wallpaper, with its patterned side rolled inward, unrolled against it. Your dealer will help you match wallpapers and pastes for both techniques.

With prepasted wallpaper, the strip also should be rolled pattern inward so the paste will be outside. Set a plastic water tray two thirds full of water on a dropcloth or towel in front of the wall; then immerse the rolled strip. The paper needs to soak for 10 to 60 seconds — as specified by the manufacturer. Grasp the strip by the top corners and slowly pull it up the wall to the ceiling, letting the excess water drip back into the box.

The other techniques of paperhanging are the same whatever the paper. Trimming, rolling seams, shaping wallpaper around doors or windows, and fitting it at corners are standard. So, too, are the tools: plumb bob and chalk line, metal yardstick, utility knife with a generous supply of replacement blades, paint roller, roller pan or water tray, smoothing brush, metal triangle or wide-blade taping knife, seam roller and sharp scissors.

Both cutting and conventional pasting call for a worktable about 6 feet long and at least as wide as the wallpaper. You can improvise with a piece of plywood set on two sawhorses or card tables, or rent a pasting table from a rental agency.

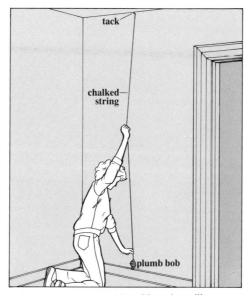

1 **Marking a vertical line.** Near the ceiling at an inside corner, measure across the right-hand wall to the width of the wallpaper minus ½ inch. Push a tack into the wall here. Pull the chalked string from a plumb bob, attach the tab at the end of the string to the tack and hold the bob away from the wall. Flick the string to remove excess chalk, then let the bob fall straight. Pull the string taut. Press the bob against the wall; snap the string, making a chalked line on the wall.

2 **Cutting the first strip.** If the pattern needs matching, unroll the wallpaper partway and hold it at the ceiling line to see where the pattern should break. With a pencil, mark this point on the back of the material. Unroll the paper face down on a worktable and — with a utility knife and a metal yardstick — cut it 2 inches above the mark. From the mark, cut a strip of wall height plus 2 more inches. For other patterns, cut a strip 4 inches longer than wall height.

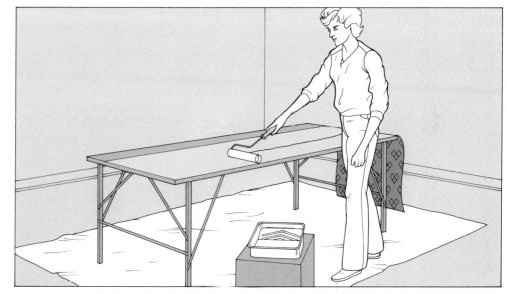

3 **Applying paste.** Pour premixed adhesive into a roller tray when you are ready to hang the wallpaper. For dry adhesive, mix it with water as the manufacturer directs. Beat the paste with a wire whisk until it is free of lumps; if necessary, strain it through cheesecloth to smooth it.

Position the wallpaper strip on the pasting table, keeping the bottom corner that is nearest you aligned with the table's edge. Using a paint roller, apply paste from about the center of the strip to the bottom and the near edge — sweeping the roller off the table at the end and side. Then slide the strip over to align with the opposite edge of the table and apply paste to the other half of the wallpaper. ▶

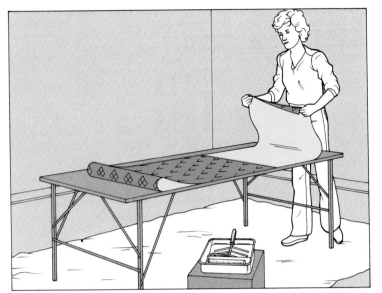

4 **Folding the strip.** When the lower two thirds of the strip is evenly coated with adhesive *(Step 3)*, pick up the end and fold the coated section in half crosswise — paste side to paste side. Technically, this manner of folding is called booking. Without creasing the fold, align the strip at the edges. Slide the folded part of the strip out of the way, then paste and fold the upper third of the strip *(above)*. Allow the pasted strip to rest for five minutes or so before you start hanging it, to give the material time to absorb the paste and become pliable.

5 **Hanging the first strip.** Unfold the upper section of the wallpaper. Grasping the strip near the top, hold it against the wall with its top 2-inch margin extending above the ceiling line, with the left-hand edge extending ½ inch onto the left wall and the right-hand edge at the chalked line on the right wall. Pat the wallpaper into place with your fingers.

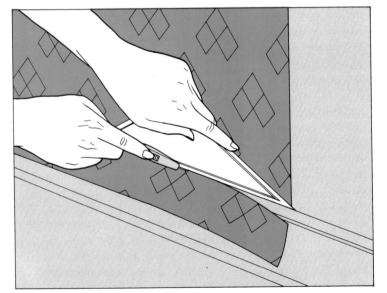

7 **Trimming the strip.** Press a metal triangle or a wide-bladed taping knife against the strip where it crosses the ceiling line. Cut off the excess wallpaper with a utility knife. Trim the wallpaper at the baseboard in the same way, as shown here. With a sponge wrung out in clear water, wipe any traces of paste from the baseboard, ceiling and wallpaper. TIP: To ensure neat edges, it is wise to change the blade in the utility knife after making every five or six cuts.

8 **Marking the next strip.** Unroll some more of the wallpaper, and hold it against the wall at the ceiling line. Butt the left-hand edge to the right-hand edge of the previous strip, then match the pattern at the ceiling. Mark the strip, and cut it to length, leaving 2-inch margins at the top and bottom of the strip as before *(Step 2)*.

   If the strip overlaps a window frame or, as shown here, a doorframe by a wide margin, mark the section you must eliminate — allowing a margin of 2 or 3 inches — and trim out the section when you cut the strip. This way, you will minimize smears on the frame when you are pasting.

6 **Brushing the strip into place.** Slit the material above the corner so that you can press the top of the strip flat *(inset)*. Then, working from the chalked line across the strip at the ceiling line, use short, upward strokes of a smoothing brush to push the wallpaper against the wall. Brushing up and out from the center, gradually work your way down the wall to smooth the top part of the strip.

Unfold the bottom of the strip and begin stroking downward, aligning the wallpaper against the chalked line as you proceed. At the baseboard, slit the material to fit it into the corner.

Finally, brush the entire strip again from top to bottom; if any wrinkle or bubble appears, gently pull the strip away from the wall there, and brush it back into place.

9 **Hanging the next strip.** Paste the strip as before and hang it, butting the edges of the two strips and matching the pattern where the edges meet. If the strip meets no obstructions, trim off the excess wallpaper at the top and bottom of the strip. If the strip must be fitted around a window or door, make a diagonal cut with scissors at the corner of the casement or molding before trimming the paper.

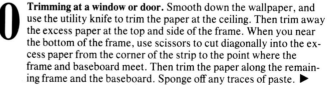

10 **Trimming at a window or door.** Smooth down the wallpaper, and use the utility knife to trim the paper at the ceiling. Then trim away the excess paper at the top and side of the frame. When you near the bottom of the frame, use scissors to cut diagonally into the excess paper from the corner of the strip to the point where the frame and baseboard meet. Then trim the paper along the remaining frame and the baseboard. Sponge off any traces of paste. ▶

11 **Rolling the seam.** Let the paste dry for about 15 minutes (you can hang another strip or two in the meantime). Then use a seam roller to press together the edges of the seam between the first two strips. Starting at the ceiling line, roll the cylinder up and down against the wallpaper, taking short strokes. Wipe the roller frequently to avoid spreading paste on the surface of the wallpaper. Finally, sponge both strips clean with clear water.

12 **Planning for a corner.** Measure from the last strip to the corner — in this case, an inside corner — in two places. Add ½ inch to the greater measurement to determine how wide the next section of wallpaper should be. Cut a strip to length in the usual way, then measure and mark the required width from the left-hand side of the wallpaper at several points along the strip. With the aid of the metal yardstick, draw a line connecting the marks. Cut the strip lengthwise, and set aside the right-hand section of the strip.

15 **Accommodating a switch.** Before papering over a switch, as shown, or an outlet, be sure the fuse that controls the current to it has been removed or the circuit breaker tripped. Unscrew, then lift off the plate. To smooth the paper over the switch, you may want to slit it to release the toggle. When the paper is hung and trimmed, cut diagonally to the corners of the recessed box. Trim away the flaps to form a rectangular hole in the wallpaper. Replace the plate before restoring the power.

13 **Fitting the corner.** Paste the left-hand part of the wallpaper; press it in place at the ceiling, letting the right-hand side extend ½ inch around the corner. With scissors, slit the paper above the corner so you can smooth the strip down. Brush to the bottom of the strip, and slit it to fit. Trim the top and bottom. At the right of the corner, along the ceiling, measure off the width of the right-hand section of wallpaper. Mark a vertical line and hang the right-hand section against the line as shown here, overlapping the margin at the corner.

14 **Completing a corner.** Trim the top and bottom edges of the right-hand section of the strip. Then, if the material is vinyl, apply seam adhesive along the top 10 or 12 inches of the margin of the left-hand strip. Smooth the adhesive with a flat-tipped stick or piece of lath. Press the edge of the right-hand section down over the adhesive. Repeat this process along the margin to the baseboard.

Covering a Soffit

1 **Wallpapering a soffit.** Matching the pattern of the wallpaper to the previous strip, if necessary, measure the height of the soffit. Add a 2-inch top margin plus enough bottom margin so the end of the strip will be out of sight under the soffit. Cut the wallpaper to this length and hang the strip. At the outside corner of the soffit, fold the top 2-inch margin down and use your brush to smooth the rest of the strip around the corner. With scissors, cut diagonally into the folded margin on both sides of the corner; discard the resulting triangle. Lift the flaps of wallpaper, and trim away the margin at the ceiling.

2 **Finishing a soffit corner.** Brush the wallpaper tight against the soffit. Then use the scissors to make two cuts from the bottom margin into the corner at an angle slightly less than 45°. Remove the resulting triangle and bring the remaining two flaps together underneath the corner so that the wallpaper conceals the bottom of the soffit there (inset). If there is too much overlap, recut the flaps. If the wallcovering is vinyl, use seam adhesive to join the flaps at the overlap. Brush the strip into place, trim it, rinse it clean and roll the seam.

Resilient tiles
for the floor

Your kitchen floor has to meet more varied demands than any other floor in your home. It should, of course, please the eye — as a leading constituent of the kitchen's decorating scheme and, in many instances, as the visual focus for the room. Because cooking requires so much standing and walking, comfort underfoot is particularly important. And a kitchen floor must be easily cleaned and resistant to stains from spattering grease and spilled food. To this list of necessary virtues you might add sound absorption, durability, simplicity of installation and moderate price.

Many types of flooring, from wood parquet to polished granite, offer one or several of these characteristics. But the material that provides the most successful combination of such qualities — and that is by far the most popular choice for kitchens — is synthetic resilient flooring.

Synthetic resilient floors resist moisture and stains, absorb sound, are easy on your feet and are less likely than harder flooring to break your dropped dishes. They can be purchased either as rolled sheets or as tiles. A 12-foot-wide sheet will provide a seamless surface for most kitchen floors, but it is cumbersome to install. Tiles — most widely available as 9-inch or 12-inch squares — are easier to work with. They also offer you the opportunity to create a unique pattern for your floor (*page 121*).

The basic substance in most resilient tiles is vinyl, a synthetic compound. Some tiles are made of pure vinyl. More common are those created from a mix of vinyl and another material, such as limestone or talc. Known as reinforced-vinyl or vinyl-composition tiles, they are less expensive than pure-vinyl tiles, and they offer excellent resistance to dirt, moisture, scuffs and dents.

Both pure-vinyl and vinyl-composition tiles are sometimes made with colors running all the way through, from the top surface to the underside; the colors virtually never wear away. Their designs are often simple. More intricate patterns are applied to resilient tiles by a photoprinting process not unlike that used for magazines or books. Designs printed this way can involve several colors and much more detail, but they can eventually be worn off. Wear can be slowed on any type of vinyl-composition tile by the addition of a glossy, no-wax finish, available at extra cost. Some tiles are embossed — stamped to give the surface a textured or carved appearance — before color is applied. If the embossed design involves narrow crevices, these tiles can be difficult to clean.

Almost all resilient tiles are available in self-adhesive form — that is, they can be simply pressed into place after peeling protective paper off their preglued backs. Generally speaking, they stick down as well and stay down as long as tiles glued by the traditional wet-cement method. However, self-adhesive tiles cost more and they are not compatible with all kinds of subfloors; ask your dealer if they would work in your kitchen. The step-by-step instructions that follow are for laying tiles by the traditional method. Except for actually spreading adhesive on the floor, though, the steps also apply to self-adhesive tiles.

In order to find out how many tiles you need, determine the square footage of your floor. If the floor is a simple rectangle, multiply its length by its width. If, like most floors, its shape is irregular, divide it into rectangular sections, find the square feet in each and add the figures.

Once you have the total number of square feet, add 5 per cent extra for trimmed edge tiles and waste. If you are using 12-inch-square tiles, the resulting figure is the number of tiles you will need. If you plan to buy 9-inch-square tiles, multiply the square footage by 1.78 before adding the 5 per cent extra. Resilient tiles are usually sold in boxes of 45, so unless you do not mind paying for a lot of tiles you will not use, beware of planning a pattern that incorporates only a few tiles of one color.

Before laying a new floor, pry off the shoe molding (or baseboard, if there is no shoe molding) with a utility bar; when you nail it back in place later, it will conceal the edges of the new flooring. A resilient floor will mimic the surface on which it is laid, so inspect the existing surface for bumps and hollows. Fill depressions with a filler recommended by your dealer. Sand away bumps if the old floor is wood, or use the technique on page 117 to remove a bump from resilient flooring. Caution: Never sand or scrape up an old resilient floor; carcinogenic asbestos fibers could be released into the air.

A checkerboard to stretch a small space

Vinyl tiles laid in a checkerboard placed diagonally to the walls rather than on the square give an illusion of space to the narrow kitchen below — an illusion furthered by the use of tiles cut from 12-inch squares into 6-inch squares. For precision, such cutting must be done by a dealer who has professional equipment. Although cutting does add to the cost, reducing the size of tiles makes them more proportionate to small rooms and more suitable for forming patterns in kitchens of any size.

Laying tiles requires care in planning if their alignment is not to appear skewed. A diagonal checked pattern is especially demanding. One line of tiles laid corner point to corner point should extend from the exact center of the main door. (The entry to this room is behind the camera; the door at the far end leads to a laundry room.) Yet the tiles should also be centered between the side walls — or, in this case, between the cabinets — so that trimmed tiles on opposite edges of the floor are fairly even in size. Try laying tiles without adhesive (overleaf) until you find the best layout for the room.

The choice of adhesive depends on the type of old floor you are laying the tiles on and whether it is above or below ground level; be sure to give your dealer this information when buying materials. You will need a notched trowel suited to that adhesive, a utility knife to cut the tiles, a chalk line and a steel square. ▶

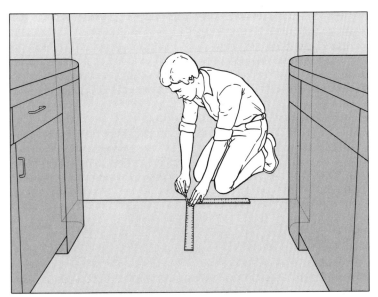

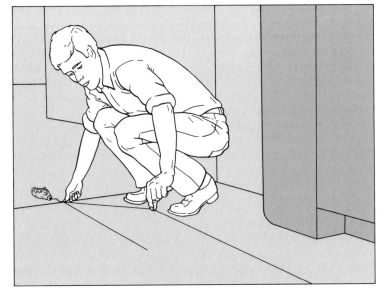

1 **Marking a start for a chalked line.** Measure the width of the main entrance to the kitchen, and mark its center point on the threshold. (If, as here, there is no threshold, draw a line across the doorway where you want the tiles to begin, and mark the center point on that line.) Use a steel square to pencil a line on the floor from the center point, perpendicular to the doorway and extending at least 2 feet into the room.

2 **Snapping a chalked line.** With a helper, stretch a chalk line (page 122) from the doorway to the opposite wall. Hold the string against the doorway center point, and direct your helper to shift the position of the other end until the string is taut and lies directly along the penciled line you drew in Step 1. Then pull the string straight up a few inches (above) and let it snap, leaving a line of powdered chalk across the floor.

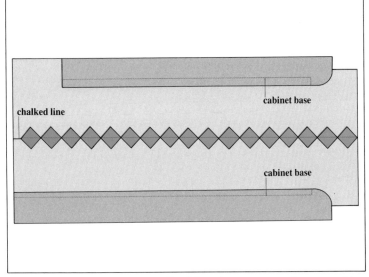

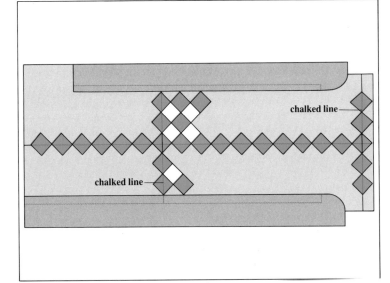

3 **Starting the dry run.** Select a tile of the color you want at the center of the doorway (at right in this drawing). Position it on the floor, one corner against the center point and the opposite corner on the chalked line. Place other tiles of the same color, corner to corner, on top of the chalked line until you reach the other side of the room and no more whole tiles will fit.

4 **Expanding the dry run.** Select appropriate places along the line of tiles to check the side-to-side results of your layout. Snap new chalked lines that run perpendicular to the primary line. Lay tiles corner to corner along these new lines; if you wish, cover a larger area with tiles for a more complete picture of what your finished floor will look like. If your dry run indicates that you will end up along a side wall with small fragments of tiles of one color and large pieces of tiles of the other color, you may want to snap a new primary chalked line at a compensating distance from the exact center of the doorway. Then try another dry run. In the room shown here, the tiles fall well-centered in the long space between the cabinets, so the primary chalked line is not moved.

Eliminating a Bump in the Old Floor

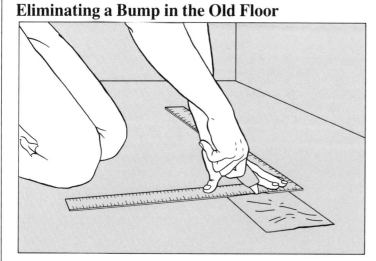

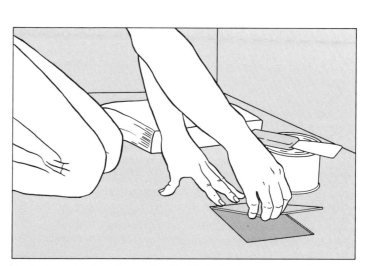

1 **Cutting around the bulge.** Before laying tiles over an old resilient floor, you must rid the surface of any bulges. The usual cause for a bulge is that the flooring has come unglued at that place. To lay it flat again, first use a utility knife and a straightedge to cut a rectangle in the flooring that encompasses the bulging area. Then lift the piece out.

2 **Regluing the piece.** Scrape the old, dried adhesive out of the hole and off the back of the cutout section of flooring with an old chisel. Then spread new adhesive — a type your dealer says is appropriate for bonding the old flooring to the subfloor — in the hole. Replace the piece in its original position — trimming the edges of the hole if the piece has expanded — and press it down. Wipe away any excess adhesive and leave a flat, heavy weight on the patch while the adhesive dries.

5 **Spreading the adhesive.** Pick up the tiles used for the dry run. Read the manufacturer's directions to find how long the adhesive should remain on the floor before tiles are laid and how long you have before it gets too dry to work with. Estimate what area you can cover with tiles in that time. Caution: Be conservative in your first estimate; if the work goes fast, you can later start spreading adhesive over larger areas.

Use a trowel with notches that match the specifications given in the directions for the adhesive. Pour a small amount of the adhesive onto the floor near the far limits of the area to be covered. Holding the trowel at an angle as shown, spread the adhesive evenly with a sweeping motion, working back toward the spot where you will lay your first tile. Spread the adhesive just up to, but not over, the primary chalked line. ▶

6 **Laying the first tile.** Hold a tile so that one corner touches the point in the doorway where the primary chalked line begins. The opposite corner should be suspended directly above the chalked line. Let that corner drop straight down onto the adhesive. If the corner does not fall precisely on the chalked line, nudge the tile into place. But try to avoid such horizontal movement of tiles; adhesive may crest up onto the edges.

7 **Working across the floor.** Using the same technique, lay a second tile — the same color as the first — to the right of the first. One corner should touch the right-hand corner of the first tile and an adjacent corner should abut the threshold — or, as here, the line across the doorway. Lay a third tile to the left of the first. Then drop two whole tiles of the other color into the triangular spaces formed by the far edges of the first three tiles. Continue to lay tiles over the area covered by adhesive, taking advantage of the edges of tiles already in place to position the one you are laying. Fill in the triangular gaps at the doorway with tiles that you cut in half, using a straightedge and a utility knife. Spread adhesive over an adjacent floor area and continue laying tiles.

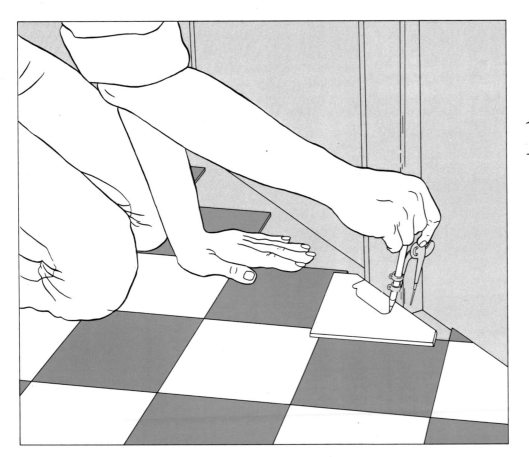

10 **Scribing around obstacles.** To fit a tile against an irregularly shaped obstacle — here, a doorjamb — first trim the tile so that it would fit the space if the obstacle were not there. Put the cut tile against the obstacle, keeping its edges parallel to the corresponding edges of adjacent tiles and its corners lined up with their corners, as shown. Set the legs of a compass to a distance equal to the greatest thickness of the obstacle. Keeping the compass legs perpendicular to the cut edge of the tile, scribe an outline of the obstacle onto the tile. Cut along the outline.
TIP: The tiles can be cut with heavy-duty scissors if they are first placed one at a time in a warm — not hot — oven for a minute, or until they have softened slightly but are not too hot to hold.

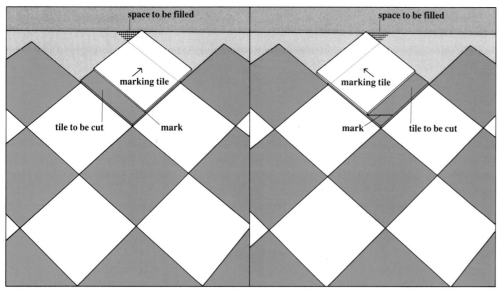

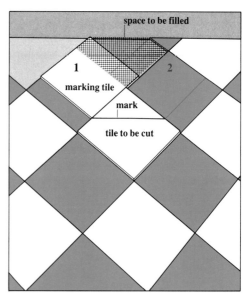

8 **Making a triangular piece.** Along a wall you may need to fill a triangular space *(crosshatched area)* smaller than a half tile. Place the tile to be cut — here, a dark one — over the adjoining already-laid tile of the same color and align their edges. Set a third tile — here, a light one is used — on top to serve as a marking tile. Slide the marking tile diagonally toward the right *(above, left)*, keeping the edges aligned. (For clarity, the adhesive is not shown.) When its leading corner touches the wall, mark where the opposite corner rests on the tile to be cut. Return the marking tile to its original position, and slide it to the left *(above, right)*. When it touches the wall, mark where its opposite corner lies. Cut the sandwiched tile along a straight line connecting the two marks.

9 **Filling a pentagonal edge space.** Set the tile to be cut atop the adjacent tile of the same color. Place a marking tile in position **1** above — side to side with the tile to be cut and with one corner against the wall. Mark where the opposite corner touches the tile to be cut. Move the marking tile to position **2** and mark where its corner touches the tile to be cut. Draw a line between the two marks; cut along this line to make a piece that fills the space.

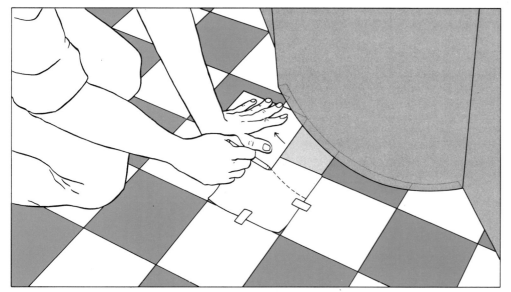

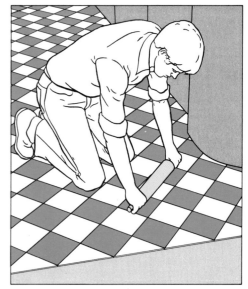

11 **Fitting tiles under low overhangs.** If a tile needs to slip beneath a low overhang, such as the bottom lip of this curved cabinet, tape a tile-sized square of paper to the adjoining whole tile of the other color. Place a marking tile atop the paper square. Push the marking tile straight under the overhang until one corner hits the unseen obstacle; mark where its adjacent corner lies on the paper square. Keeping the marking tile's edges parallel to the edges of already-laid tiles, slide it along the obstacle, using its corner as a guide for marking the corresponding curve on the paper. Cut a tile to the shape of the resulting template, and slip it under the overhang.

12 **Rolling the tiles.** If the manufacturer recommends it, roll the laid tiles to ensure a firm bond. Use a sturdy rolling pin, and press straight down. If adhesive has oozed up between tiles, do not roll over it; wipe it off with a clean rag and a solvent suggested by its manufacturer.

At a doorway without a threshold, use a metal edge strip to cover the edge of the tiles. Cut the strip with a hacksaw, and fix it to the subfloor with screws. ▶

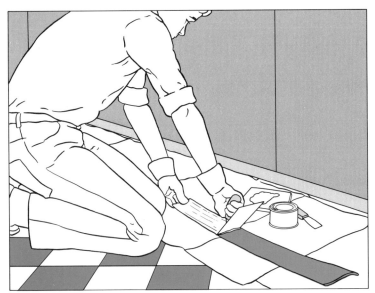

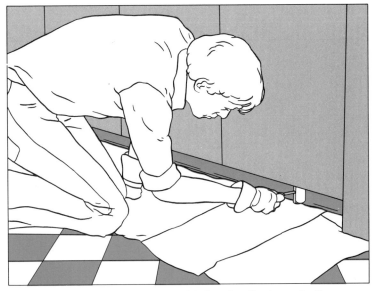

13 Covering edges with vinyl molding. To install vinyl cove molding against your cabinet toekick, first cut the molding to length with a utility knife. Lay the strip of molding, backside up, on newspapers. Using an adhesive and trowel recommended by the dealer or manufacturer, spread adhesive on most of the back of the molding. Leave all of the curved portion at the bottom of the molding and a ¼-inch-wide strip at the top free of adhesive.

14 Fixing the molding to the toekick. Let the adhesive set for the length of time recommended by the manufacturer. When the adhesive is ready, position the molding on the cabinet toekick. Press the molding hard against the toekick with a small roller *(above)*.

Laying Tiles on the Square

Instead of laying tiles diagonally, as in the foregoing example, you may want to set their edges parallel to your kitchen walls. Both the planning and the actual installation will be considerably simpler if you do.

When tiles are laid squared to the walls, positioning tiles in doorways is generally considered less important than placing the center of the pattern at or near the center of the room. The steps at right show how to accomplish this with chalked lines and dry runs.

Trimming tiles to fit rectangular spaces along the walls is much easier than cutting triangular and pentagonal pieces for the edges of a diagonal layout. Simply place the tile to be cut on top of the last whole tile in the row, aligning their edges. Set a marking tile atop those two, and slide it until its leading edge butts the wall. Using the overlapping edge of the marking tile as a guide, draw a line across the tile to be cut; then cut along that line.

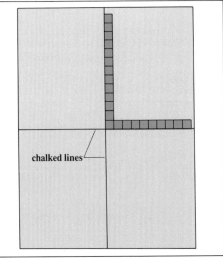

chalked lines

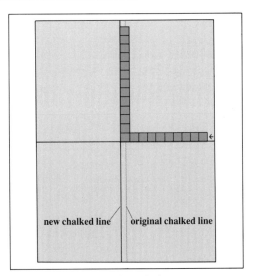

new chalked line   original chalked line

1 Laying a dry run. By measuring, locate the centers of the four sides of the room. Snap two crossed chalked lines *(page 116, Step 2)* that connect the centers of opposite sides. Use a steel square to determine whether the lines are perpendicular. If they are not, replace one line with a new line that is perpendicular to the other. (The result will be edge tiles that are not perfect rectangles along two walls.) Now lay out a dry run of two rows of whole tiles, as shown.

2 Shifting a line. At the end of a row, measure the distance between the wall and the nearest edge of the last tile. If the distance is less than half a tile width, snap a new chalked line parallel to the line from which the row started and half a tile width closer to the opposite wall. Check the border of the other row the same way.

When laying the tiles in adhesive, begin at the intersection of the chalked lines, and cover one quadrant at a time.

Designing Your Own Tile Floor

Tiles have an especially appealing virtue: With some imagination and a bit of preliminary planning on graph paper, you can create a one-of-a-kind kitchen floor with resilient tiles. Out of countless possibilities, the patterns here illustrate four. In this case, the patterns in the top row are overall designs that are meant to be repeated across the floor, while the bottom patterns are feature designs for the center of the floor.

To fashion a special pattern in tile, first consider the shape and the size of the area it is to fill. Try to proportion the design to the space. When selecting colors, take into account not only how they will contrast or blend with kitchen walls, but also how they affect the colors of cabinets, appliances, even knobs. And consider the impact of walls and floors in neighboring rooms that are visible from the kitchen.

When you have a notion of the colors and general pattern you want, make a plan of the kitchen floor on graph paper. Each square can represent one tile, as in these patterns, or, if you are planning a complex layout that involves cut sec-tions of tiles, you may want to have four graph-paper squares equal a whole tile. Keep experimenting with arrangements on the graph paper until you achieve the design you want.

If you can, buy tiles from a dealer who is willing to take them back if you return them clean and undamaged in their boxes. Lay the tiles out on the floor in an extensive dry run *(pages 116 and 120)* to make sure you like the pattern and colors. During the dry run and the installation, keep the graph-paper plan handy so you can refer to it as you go along.

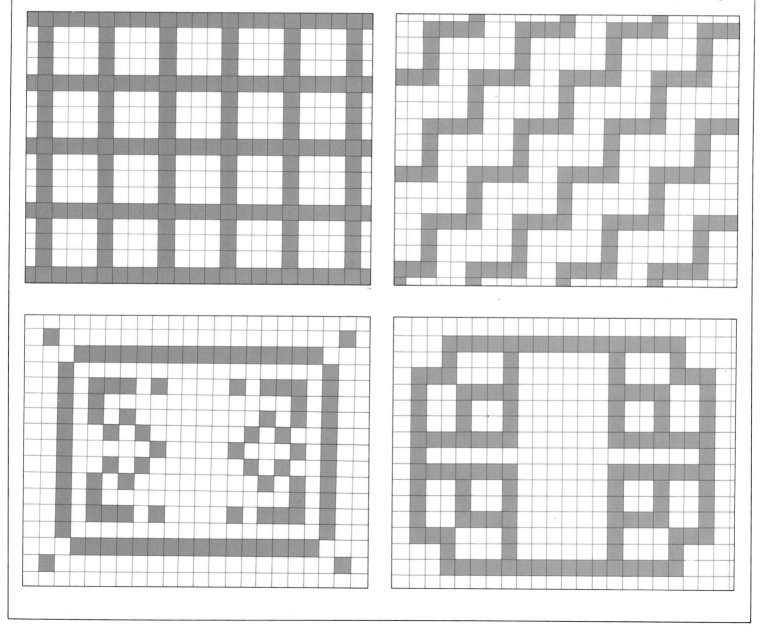

A selection of essential hand tools

When selecting even the simplest of hand tools, quality should be your guide. Shop at a hardware store where the selection is large and the staff is well informed. Choose tools in the medium to high price range. The extra expense can mean the difference between tools that never work properly and those that will provide years of precision performance.

You should have a 24-inch metal carpenter's level and some type of steel square that both measures linear distances and checks 90° angles. A chalk line/plumb bob is handy for jobs like wallpapering; it indicates vertical lines and marks them on the wall.

Although power saws *(opposite and pages 124-125)* generally make faster cuts with much less effort, a crosscut saw *(right)* is useful for rough work and when few cuts are required. Look for a 26-inch blade with 10 or 12 teeth per inch; it makes fairly smooth cuts in plywood and boards. The blade should be taper-ground—thicker near the teeth than at the top—to reduce friction and binding during the cut.

A more specialized tool combination —the backsaw and miter box *(pages 28-29)*—cuts finer edges and precise 45° and 90° angles on moldings and narrow boards. Whatever the kind of saw, have a tool-repair shop keep the blade sharpened. And always cut on a steady surface, anchoring your work with C clamps whenever possible.

A curved-claw hammer is for driving and pulling out nails. Its head should weigh about 16 ounces and be made of drop-forged steel. The ball-peen hammer is for striking metal objects other than nails—metal punches, for example *(page 63)*. It has a specially tempered head, which should weigh about 20 ounces. For safety, keep hammer heads clean and free from oil or grease, which might cause them to glance off a struck surface.

Two flat-tipped screwdrivers, one with a ¼-inch-wide blade and one with a 5/16-inch-wide blade, will fit the most commonly used single-slot screws—those that range in size from No. 6 to No. 12. Nos. 1 and 2 Phillips screwdrivers will fit most Phillips, or cross-slot, screws. Wood or plastic handles with wide, rounded ribs or plastic handles with rubber grips are the most comfortable to use.

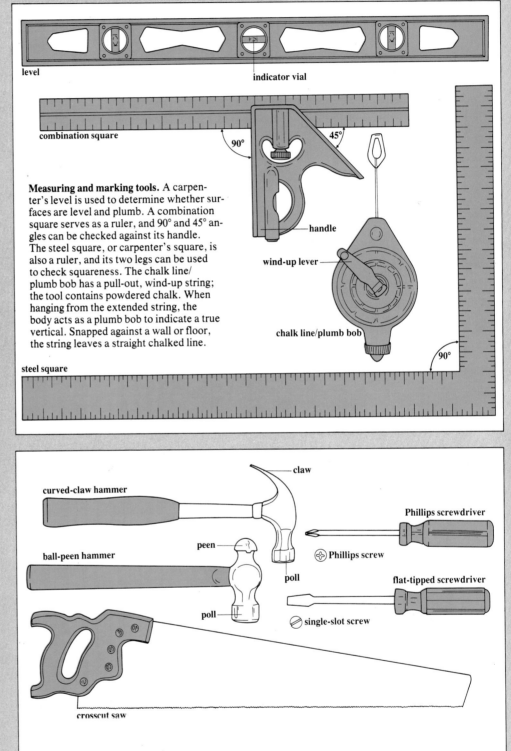

level

indicator vial

combination square

90°   45°

handle

wind-up lever

chalk line/plumb bob

steel square

90°

Measuring and marking tools. A carpenter's level is used to determine whether surfaces are level and plumb. A combination square serves as a ruler, and 90° and 45° angles can be checked against its handle. The steel square, or carpenter's square, is also a ruler, and its two legs can be used to check squareness. The chalk line/plumb bob has a pull-out, wind-up string; the tool contains powdered chalk. When hanging from the extended string, the body acts as a plumb bob to indicate a true vertical. Snapped against a wall or floor, the string leaves a straight chalked line.

claw

curved-claw hammer

Phillips screwdriver

peen

ball-peen hammer

poll

Phillips screw

poll

flat-tipped screwdriver

poll

single-slot screw

crosscut saw

Simple hand tools. A crosscut saw cuts across the grain of boards and, more slowly, cuts through plywood. Use the poll of a curved-claw hammer to drive nails, the claw to pry them out. The flat-faced poll of a ball-peen hammer is used for hitting metal objects such as punches; the less frequently used round peen originally was designed for rounding off rivet heads. The flat-tipped screwdriver drives standard single-slot screws, and the Phillips screwdriver drives cross-slot Phillips screws.

Power tools for ease and precision

Small power tools are indispensable aids to a home decorator. If purchased wisely and handled properly, the tools on these pages will ensure even the novice of swift and professional-looking results.

In general, inferior tools will produce inferior work no matter how experienced the operator may be. When you are shopping for power tools, pass by the least expensive ones. At most hardware stores and home-improvement centers, you should be able to find moderately priced tools of medium to high quality. Look especially for such features as heavy-duty electrical cords that will withstand the wear and tear power tools get, permanently lubricated bearings that simplify tool maintenance, and double-insulated plastic bodies that eliminate the need for having a grounded power cord with a three-pronged plug.

Every bit as important as buying the right tools is using the right tool for the job. A saber saw, for example, is designed for cutting curves *(below)*; although it can make a long, straight cut through plywood, the straight cut will be cleaner and more precise if it is done with a circular saw instead *(overleaf)*. All power tools come with manufacturer's instructions for care and handling. Take the time to read the instructions, then practice with the tools before you begin a project. Familiarity will lead to easy and proficient handling.

Safety is as important as skill in the operation of power tools, and a few rules apply in every situation:

• Dress for the job. Avoid loose clothing, tuck in your shirt, and roll up your sleeves. Tie back your hair if it is long. And wear goggles when there is a possibility that dust or shavings will fly into your eyes — for example, whenever you are cutting with a circular saw or when you are drilling at eye level or overhead. Do not wear gloves when operating power tools; gloves reduce dexterity and can catch in moving parts.

• When operating a power tool, be sure to work on a stable surface; clamp the work to the surface whenever practical.

• Stand comfortably, do not reach any farther than you easily can, and never stand directly in front of — or directly behind — a moving saw blade. Circular saws have a tendency to kick back toward the operator if the blade gets jammed in the middle of a cut; this generally happens when the sawed section of a workpiece has not been supported as it ought to be to let the saw blade move freely. If the blade should bind while you are making a cut, switch the saw off immediately and support the work to open the cut. If you will be making long cuts in boards or plywood, recruit a helper to support the work for you.

• Always unplug power tools when they are not in use, and whenever you adjust or change parts.

The Saber Saw

Because the blade of the saber saw is only about ¼ inch wide, it can be maneuvered through tight spots and intricate, curved cuts without binding or breaking. With straight cuts, the narrow blade tends to wander from a guideline. But a straight-edged guide clamped to the work *(overleaf)* makes such cuts relatively straight.

Your best buy is a variable-speed saw with a trigger switch *(right)*. You can speed it up along broad curves and slow down for tricky areas by altering pressure on the trigger. Blades come in sets and individually. Most will cut through wood up to 2 inches thick. Blades with six teeth per inch make fast, rough cuts; blades with 10 to 14 teeth per inch cut more slowly, but also more cleanly. For fine cuts in plywood, buy taper-ground blades with 10 teeth per inch.

To ensure a smooth cut on the good face of a board or panel, work with that surface down. The saber-saw blade cuts on the upstroke, sometimes tearing slivers from the top surface of the work.

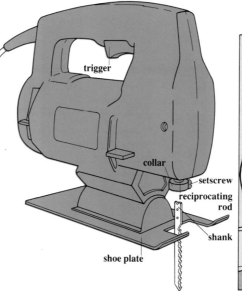

A variable-speed saber saw. A trigger mounted in the handle lets you turn the saw on and off as you wish and regulate the speed with which it cuts. To insert a blade, loosen the setscrew in the collar on the reciprocating rod; you will need a screwdriver or a hex wrench, depending on the saw model. Push the notched shank of the blade as far as it will go up into the hollow portion of the reciprocating rod, then retighten the setscrew to anchor the blade.

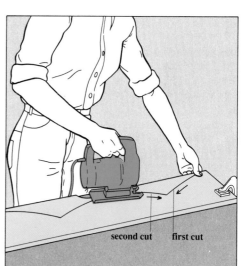

Cutting a curved pattern. Plan your cuts so you will not force the blade through an impossibly tight turn; here, the first and second cuts both move toward a sharp corner. Rest the tip of the shoe plate on the wood. Start the saw, and guide the blade into the wood, swinging the back of the saw right or left as you move into curves. Do not force the blade, lest it bind or break. If you end a cut with the blade in the wood, let the blade stop completely before withdrawing it.

The Circular Saw

The 7¼-inch circular saw, named for the diameter of its blade, is a good size for home use. It will cut through lumber up to 2 inches thick at any angle from 45° to 90°.

Many 7¼-inch blades are available; for the projects in this book, the plywood blade *(right)* and crosscut blade *(inset)* are most useful. The former cuts plywood with a minimum of splintering; the latter makes clean cuts across boards. In either case, cut with the good surface of the work facing down; the saw's blade cuts upward, leaving splinters along the top of the cut edge.

A circular saw can be guided accurately freehand for short cuts; for longer cuts, use a guide *(below, right)*. The manufactured edge of ¼-inch plywood makes a good, straight guide. Clamp it where the lumber is supported from below, and work the saw so that its motor passes over the guide: A ¼-inch piece of plywood leaves plenty of clearance. If you push the motor over unsupported wood, the board or panel may crack.

Keeping a firm grip is very important with a circular saw; a 7¼-inch model can weigh 10 pounds. Many saws have an extra handle for an optional two-handed grip. Whether you use one hand or two, be ready to support the weight of the saw as it emerges from a finished cut.

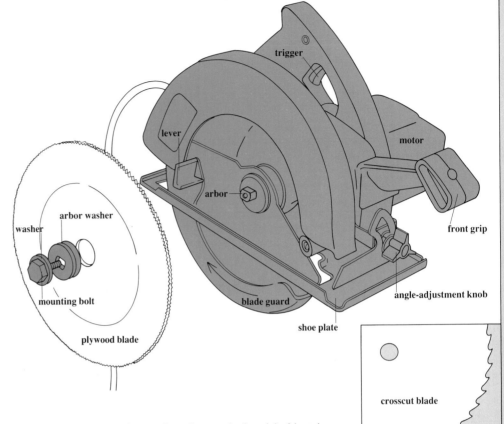

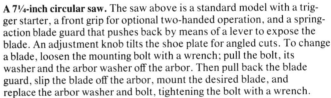

A 7¼-inch circular saw. The saw above is a standard model with a trigger starter, a front grip for optional two-handed operation, and a spring-action blade guard that pushes back by means of a lever to expose the blade. An adjustment knob tilts the shoe plate for angled cuts. To change a blade, loosen the mounting bolt with a wrench; pull the bolt, its washer and the arbor washer off the arbor. Then pull back the blade guard, slip the blade off the arbor, mount the desired blade, and replace the arbor washer and bolt, tightening the bolt with a wrench.

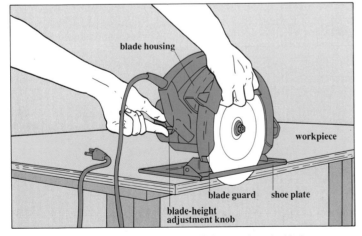

Adjusting the depth of the cut. For most efficient cutting, the blade ought to extend ¼ inch below the bottom surface of the workpiece. To raise or lower the blade, lay the saw's shoe plate flat on the surface of the wood, loosen the blade-height adjustment knob and push the blade guard up to expose the blade. With one hand, hold the blade guard in its raised position while grasping the blade housing to support the saw body. Keeping the shoe plate flat on the wood, raise or lower the saw body — and with it the blade — until the blade is in the proper position. Then tighten the adjustment knob again.

Making a straight cut. Clamp a guide strip of ¼-inch plywood to the work at a distance from the cutting line equal to the distance between the blade and the outer edge of the wide section of the shoe plate. To start the cut, rest the shoe plate against the strip; align the blade with the cutting line, but do not let the blade touch the edge of the work. Grip the saw with one hand or two, whichever is more comfortable for you, then press the trigger and push the blade steadily into the work. As the cut nears completion, have your helper hold the sawed portion to keep it from falling and splintering the panel.

The Variable-Speed Drill

As its name implies, the variable-speed drill works at a variety of speeds, depending on how hard you squeeze its trigger. Small holes in wood are bored at the fastest speeds; slower speeds are better for drilling large holes in wood and for any hole in metal or masonry.

The drill at right is a ⅜-inch model, which can accommodate bit shanks from ¹⁄₆₄ inch to ⅜ inch in diameter. Within that range, a wide assortment of bits is available to drill holes from ¹⁄₆₄ inch to 1½ inches in diameter in wood, metal or masonry.

For most of the projects in this volume, twist bits are used to drill pilot holes in wood — holes to receive the threaded portions of wood screws. Charts listing the bit used to make pilot holes for each screw size are available at hardware stores.

When a hole in wood will receive the unthreaded shank and the head of a screw as well as the threads, an adjustable counterbore bit will drill a hole that accommodates all three sections of the screw. (One bit generally can be used for three consecutive screw sizes.) Follow the manufacturer's instructions to adjust the movable sections of the bit to your specifications.

Spade bits bore holes up to 1½ inches in diameter; because these bits tend to wobble and are difficult to guide straight by hand, use of a drill guide is advisable. The model at right, below, will fit any drill with a threaded shaft and is available wherever drills are sold.

Masonry bits, with closely spaced, carbide-tipped edges, grind slowly through brick and concrete, which would crumble under a twist bit.

Bits are available in most hardware stores. Twist bits often are sold in sets that include the most frequently used sizes. Buy additional sizes and types as you need them for particular projects.

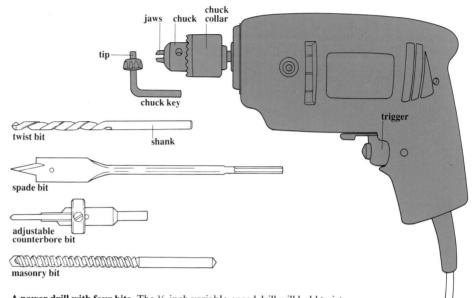

A power drill with four bits. The ⅜-inch variable-speed drill will hold twist, spade, counterbore and masonry bits with shanks up to ⅜ inch in diameter. To insert a bit, turn the collar of the chuck to open the jaws, push the bit shank between the jaws and tighten the collar by hand until the jaws grip the shank. Then push the tip of the chuck key into each of the three holes in the chuck in turn, and twist the key handle. To exchange bits, you will need the chuck key to loosen the collar before you can turn it by hand.

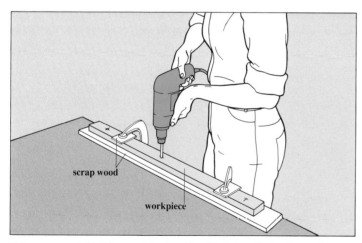

Using a power drill. After marking locations for holes, fasten the work with C clamps to a table; set pieces of scrap wood between the jaws of the clamps and the work, and beneath the work to protect the table. Hold the drill with both hands, the forefinger of one hand poised to press the trigger and the other hand holding the body of the drill. Set the tip of the bit on the work, squeeze the trigger and push the bit straight into the wood; use steady, moderate pressure. If the bit skips off the work, tap a nail into the starting point to make an indentation for the tip of the bit.

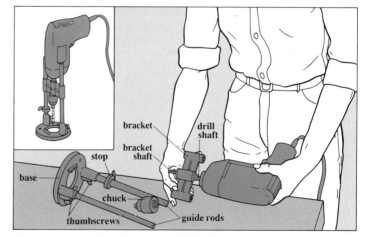

Attaching a drill guide. Remove the drill's chuck. (Most unscrew from the shaft of the drill, but check the manufacturer's instructions.) Twist the guide bracket onto the drill shaft; screw the chuck onto the bracket's shaft. Slip the guide rods through their holes in the bracket, loosen the thumbscrews on the base, set the ends of the rods flush with the bottom of the base, and tighten the screws; this procedure ensures that the holes drilled are perpendicular to the work surface when the drill guide is upright *(inset)*. If you want to drill to a certain depth, position the stop on the guide rod after you have inserted a bit in the chuck.

Acknowledgments

The index for this book was prepared by Linda Busetti. The editors wish to thank the following persons and institutions: Steve Aldrich, Grants Pass, Oregon; Roswell W. Ard, Traverse City, Michigan; David A. Bennett, Alexandria, Virginia; Pat Bergeron, Monrovia, Maryland; Gianni Braghieri, Milan; Emmett Bright, Rome; Jack Callahan, Yorktowne Inc., Red Lion, Pennsylvania; Robert C. de Camara, Armstrong World Industries, Inc., Lancaster, Pennsylvania; Sharon Clarke-Fodor, L. E. Carpenter Design Center, Milford, Connecticut; Judy Cody, The Gallery at Workbench, New York; William R. Crawford, Peix and Crawford Architecture, New York; Walter T. Davis, Formica Products Research Center, Cincinnati, Ohio; Carla De Benedetti, Milan; Pierre Deux Ltd., New York; Alexandra Eames, Sag Harbor, New York; James and Richard Edwards, Custom Laminated Furniture, Lorton, Virginia; Charlotte Farber, Jahreszeiten Verlag, Hamburg; Joël Féau, Paris; Richard Hall, Wallcovering Information Bureau, Springfield, New Jersey; Neal Holzman, Sanitas Division, L. E. Carpenter & Company, Wharton, New Jersey; Joseph A. Hoover, Capital-Asam, Inc., Washington, D.C.; L. E. Hopkins, Corian Building Products Group, E. I. du Pont de Nemours & Company Inc., Wilmington, Delaware; Robert Kleinhans, Tile Council of America, Princeton, New Jersey; Carl Lang, Sanitas Division, L. E. Carpenter & Company, Wharton, New Jersey; George Lavenburg, Ceramic Tile Institute, Los Angeles, California; Douglas McGlinchey, American Olean Tile Co., Lansdale, Pennsylvania; Win Nevins, Duron Paints and Wallcoverings, Alexandria, Virginia; John Nichols, Porter-Cable Inc., Jackson, Tennessee; J. D. Olson, Stanley Tools, New Britain, Connecticut; Cynthia Patterson, Taos Clay Products, Taos, New Mexico; J. Douglas Peix, Peix and Crawford Architecture, New York; Rod Rhodes, Bath and Kitchen House, Falls Church, Virginia; Luke and Nancy Rowe, Rawlings Floor Covering Inc., Alexandria, Virginia; Frederick W. Sachs Jr., Smoot Lumber Co., Alexandria, Virginia; Joseph Schifflett, Building & Mechanical Inspection Department, Alexandria, Virginia; Michael Schimmel, RXXs Chemical, Dearborn, Michigan; Peter Schreck, Rome; Susan T. Van Voorhees, American Olean Tile Co., Lansdale, Pennsylvania; Stan Warshaw, United States School of Professional Paperhanging Inc., Rutland, Vermont; Deborah Wilson, L. E. Carpenter Design Center, Milford, Connecticut.

Picture Credits

The sources for the photographs in this book are listed below, followed by the sources for the illustrations. Credits from left to right on a single page or a two-page spread are separated by semicolons; credits from top to bottom are separated by dashes.

Photographs: **Cover:** Lisl Dennis, photographer / Carolyn Fleig, stylist. **2:** Robert Perron, photographer / Ric Weinshenk, architect. **3:** Tim Street-Porter from Elizabeth Whiting Associates, London, photographer / design by Mark Meryash. **4, 5:** Studio Azzuro, Milan, photographer / Studio MORSA, architects. **6:** Aldo Ballo, Milan, photographer / Gianni Braghieri, architect. **7:** Norman McGrath, photographer / design by Florence Perchuk & Associates: chair, table settings by Pierre Deux, New York. **8, 9:** Norman McGrath, photographer / design by Laura Odell-Kitchen Designs; Alan Jay, photographer / design by Charles Morris Mount, Inc.: high-gloss Formica® laminate from the Design Concepts Collection. **22:** Lisl Dennis, photographer. **24:** Dan Cunningham, photographer. **25:** Robert Perron, photographer. **26:** John Neubauer, photographer, courtesy Rector Associates, Alexandria, Virginia. **29:** John Neubauer, photographer. **30, 32:** Dan Cunningham, photographer. **33:** Elizabeth Whiting Associates, London, photographer. **42:** Dan Cunningham, photographer. **46, 50:** John Neubauer, photographer. **54:** John Burwell, photographer. **61:** Dan Cunningham, photographer. **70:** Dan Cunningham, photographer, courtesy Harbor Terrace Apartments, Alexandria, Virginia. **77:** Dan Cunningham, photographer. **78:** John Neubauer, photographer. **84, 85:** Lisl Dennis, photographer / Carolyn Fleig, stylist. **93:** John Neubauer, photographer. **94, 95:** Lisl Dennis, photographer / Patricia Carpenter, stylist. **103:** Dan Cunningham, photographer. **108:** Robert Perron, photographer. **115:** Robert Perron, photographer / Peix & Crawford, architects.

Illustrations: **15-17:** Sketches by George Bell, inked by Frederic F. Bigio from B-C Graphics. **18, 19:** Sketches by George Bell, inked by Walter Hilmers Jr. from HJ Commercial Art. **20, 21:** Sketches by Fred Holz, inked by Walter Hilmers Jr. from HJ Commercial Art. **23-25:** Sketches by William J. Hennessy Jr., inked by John Massey. **27-29:** Sketches by William J. Hennessy Jr., inked by Adisai Hemintranont from Sai Graphis. **30-32:** Sketches by Jack Arthur, inked by Adisai Hemintranont from Sai Graphis. **33-35:** Sketches by George Bell, inked by Frederic F. Bigio from B-C Graphics. **36:** Sketches by Fred Holz, inked by Frederic F. Bigio from B-C Graphics. **37-41:** Sketches by Fred Holz, inked by Walter Hilmers Jr. from HJ Commercial Art. **43-45:** Sketches by Jack Arthur, inked by Eduino J. Pereira. **47-49:** Sketches by Fred Holz, inked by Frederic F. Bigio from B-C Graphics. **51-53:** Sketches by George Bell, inked by Elsie J. Hennig. **55-60:** Sketches by William J. Hennessy Jr., inked by Eduino J. Pereira. **62, 63:** Sketches by George Bell, inked by Elsie J. Hennig. **65-69:** Sketches by Joan McGurren, inked by Frederic F. Bigio from B-C Graphics. **71-75:** Sketches by George Bell, inked by Eduino J. Pereira. **76, 77:** Sketches by George Bell, inked by Stephen A. Turner. **79-81:** Sketches by Roger Essley, inked by Elsie J. Hennig. **83:** Sketch by Fred Holz, inked by Walter Hilmers Jr. from HJ Commercial Art. **85-93:** Sketches by Jack Arthur, inked by William J. Hennessy Jr. **95-101:** Sketches by Fred Holz, inked by John Massey. **104-107:** Sketches by Fred Holz, inked by Frederic F. Bigio from B-C Graphics. **109-113:** Sketches by Fred Holz, inked by John Massey. **116-125:** Sketches by Roger Essley, inked by Adisai Hemintranont from Sai Graphis.

Index

A

Alkyd paints, 14, 22, 102, 103
Anchor fastener, 39
Appliances: location of, 16-19; measuring during planning, 67; removing, 70

B

Backsaw, and miter box, 28, 29, 122
Backsplash: covering with plastic laminate, 100; making with tile, 91
Ball-peen hammer, 61, 63, 122
Base cabinets, 64-66; installing, 70-75; removing, 71. See also Cabinets
Beading, in painting, 103, 104
Bending brass rods, 45
Bleaching wood, 25
Blind corner cabinets, 65, 66
Bolts, types of, 40-41
Brushes, for paint, 22, 24
Building codes, 19
Butcher-block counters, 80-81, 82. See also Countertops

C

Cabinets: attaching adjacent, 75, 77; on casters, 78-81; choosing, 64, 79; corner configurations, 66, 67; fluorescent lights underneath, 20, 33-35; hardware for, 26-27; installing, 70-77; molding on, 28-29; mounting, 73, 76-77; painting, 22-24; planning for, 67-69; platform for, 75; refurbishing, 14; removing, 71; staining and varnishing, 25; storage devices for, 20; stripes on, 24; stripping, 20, 25; types of, 64-66
Carpenter's level, 71, 72, 122
Carpenter's square, 43, 122
Casters, attaching to cabinets, 80
Ceiling hook, 40
Ceiling lag shield, 40
Ceiling-mounted pot rack, 61-63
Ceramic tile, 82; installing, 84-93; painting, 92-93
Chalk line/plumb bob, 21, 122
China paint, for tile, 92, 93
Circular saw, 124
Cleats, 76-77
Color-cored laminate, 83
Combination square, 122
Cookbook holder, 20
Cooking center, 14, 17
Corner base filler, 75
Corner cabinets, 66, 67; installing, 72, 77. See also Cabinets
Counterbore bit: adjustable, 125; use of, 59
Countertops: applying ceramic tile to, 84-93; attaching new, 74; choosing, 82-83; covering with plastic laminate, 94-101; heights of, 15-16, 75; removing, 71
Crosscut saw, 122
Curved-claw hammer, 122

D

Dead corner, treatment of, 66, 75
Door and doorframe, painting, 107
Doors, cabinet: hardware for, 26-27; painting, 24; removing, 23
Dowels, 31; rack built of, 54-60
Drawers, 20; on glides, 21; hardware for, 26-27; preparing for painting, 23
Drill, variable-speed, 125
Drill guide, 125
Drilling, 21, 26, 27; to determine wall type, 38

E

Edge banding, ironing onto plywood, 59
Electrical systems, 19. See also Lighting, fluorescent
Ergonomics, defined, 15
Expansion shield, 40
Eye bolt, 40

F

Fasteners, types and uses of, chart 38, 39-41. See also individual entries
Filler strip, use of, 66, 72-73, 75
Flooring, 114-121; designing tile pattern for, 121; eliminating bulge in resilient tile, 117; installing resilient tile, 114-120; types of, 114
Floor plan, 67-69. See also Work centers; Planning

G

Galley kitchen, defined, 18
Glide-out units, 21
Grouting of ceramic tile, 92

H

Hacksaw, 61, 62
Hammers, types of, 122
Hanger bolt, 40
Hanger plates, attaching, 49
Hangers. See Fasteners, types and uses of
Hardware, cabinet, 20, 23; installing, 26-27; removing paint from, 25
Hardwood, described, 41
Hooks, 45. See also Ceiling hook

I

Island, rolling, 78-81

J

Jambs, painting of, 106
Jigs, for drilling, 26, 27
Joists, locating, 36

K

Knobs and handles. See Hardware, cabinet

L

Lag bolt, 40
Laminate. See Plastic laminate
Latex paints, 22, 102, 103
Lath rack, 42-45
Layout: of ceramic tile, 85-89; of resilient tile, 115-116, 120, 121. See also Floor plan; Planning; Work centers
Lazy susan, in cabinet, 21, 65, 66
Level, carpenter's, 71, 72, 122
Lighting, fluorescent, under cabinets, 20, 33-35
L kitchen, defined, 18
Load, determining proper hanger for, chart 38
Lumber, buying, 41

M

Mastic, 87
Miter box, use of, 28, 29, 122
Molding: on cabinet fronts, 20, 28-29; at floor line, 74, 120
Molly bolt®, 41
Movable cabinets, 78-81

O

Open-storage units, 36, 42-63
Orbital sander, 22, 23

P

Painting: of cabinets, 22-24; of ceiling, 104; of ceramic tile, 93; of door, 107; of room, 102-107; of sash windows, 106; stripes on cabinets, 24; of woodwork, 106-107
Paint remover, 25
Picture hook, 39
Pilot holes, 49, 73
Pipes, locating, 37
Planning: for cabinets, 64-69; for hanging units, 36-39; for remodeling, 14-19; for tile floor, 115-116, 120, 121; for tiling counters, 82-83
Plant shelves, 50-53
Plastic laminate, 83; filling cracks, 101; installing, 94-101
Plumb bob. See Chalk line/plumb bob
Plumbing renovation, 19
Plywood, types of, 41, 54
Point of first use, defined, 16
Post-formed laminate counters, 82
Pot rack, ceiling-mounted, 61-63
Power saws, 122, 123, 124
Power tools, 122-125
Preparation center, 14, 15, 16

R

Racks, 36; ceiling-mounted, 61-63; of dowels, 54-60; of lath, 42-45
Remodeling cabinets, 22-27. See also Cabinets
Renovation, 19
Repairing damaged wood, 23
Resilient floors. See Flooring
Revolving shelf units, 21, 65, 66
Router, use of, 99

S

Saber saw, 123
Safety with power tools, 123
Sashes, painting of, 106
Screwdrivers, types of, 122
Screw holes, filling, 44
Screw, self-tapping, 41
Screws, types of, 39
Shelf unit, open, 46-49
Shelves, 20-21, 36; cutting out of cabinet, 21; for plants, 50-53; revolving, 21, 65, 66
Shims, defined, 70; use of, 72-73
Sink center, 14, 17
Sink opening: cutting out, 100; tiling around, 86-87
Soffit, covering with wallpaper, 113
Softwood, defined, 41
Spackling compound, applying, 104
Spice rack: on cabinet door, 30-31; in drawer, 32
Splicing wires, 35
Square, carpenter's, 43, 122
Square, combination, 122
Staining wood, 25
Steel cabinets, 64
Steel square. See Square, carpenter's
Storage space, 16; organizers for, 20-21; at point of first use, 16, 67
Stripes on cabinets, painting, 24
Stripping paint, 20, 25
Stripping wires, 35
Studs, locating, 36
Switch, installation of, 35
Synthetic marble counters, 82. See also Countertops

T

Template: for dowel rack, 56; for molding, 28
Tile, ceramic. See Ceramic tile

Tile, resilient. *See* Flooring
Toggle bolt, 41
Tools, 122-125

U
U kitchen, defined, 19

V
Variable-speed drill, 125
Varnishing, 25
Versacolor™, for ceramic tiles, 92, 93
Vinyl floor tile. *See* Flooring
Vinyl molding, 120

W
Wall cabinets, 64-66; installing, 76-77; removing,
    76. *See also* Cabinets
Wall coverings, 102-113
Wallpaper: hanging vinyl-protected, 108-113;
    matching pattern in, 102; removing old, 103;
    types of, 102
Wall type, determining, *chart* 38
Windows, painting, 106
Wiring lights, 35
Wood screws, 39
Woodwork, painting, 106-107
Work centers, 14, 17-19
Work triangles, 18-19

Time-Life Books Inc. offers a wide range of fine
recordings, including a *Big Bands* series. For subscription
information, call 1-800-621-7026, or write TIME-LIFE
MUSIC, Time & Life Building, Chicago, Illinois 60611.